Collins

NATIONAL SPACE CENTRE

SPACE TRAVELLER'S HANDBOOK

A guide for future astronauts

Published by Collins
An imprint of HarperCollins Publishers
1 Robroyston Gate, Glasgow G33 1JN

www.collins.co.uk

HarperCollins Publishers
Macken House, 39/40 Mayor Street Upper,
Dublin 1, Ireland D01 C9W8

First published 2026

Written by: Charlie Isham & Dhara Patel

Publisher: Michelle I'Anson
Project Leader: Beth Rogers
Designer: James Hunter
Typesetter: QBS
Editorial: Tracey Cowell & Louise Robb
Production: Ilaria Rovera

A catalogue record for this book is available from the British Library.

WARNING/SAFETY INSTRUCTIONS:
ALWAYS follow all the steps in each activity carefully. TAKE CARE – parents may want to take over, especially when handling hot or heavy objects, glass, scissors, knives, matches or other potentially dangerous materials. ALWAYS read the safety instructions on any products and materials used and ensure that you follow the manufacturer's guidelines and take all appropriate safety precautions.

ISBN 978-0-00-882696-3

Printed by Replika Press Pvt. Ltd., India

10 9 8 7 6 5 4 3 2 1

Collins

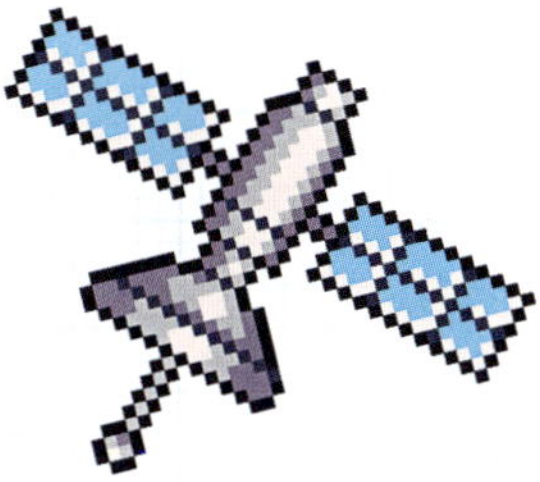

SPACE TRAVELLER'S HANDBOOK

A guide for future astronauts

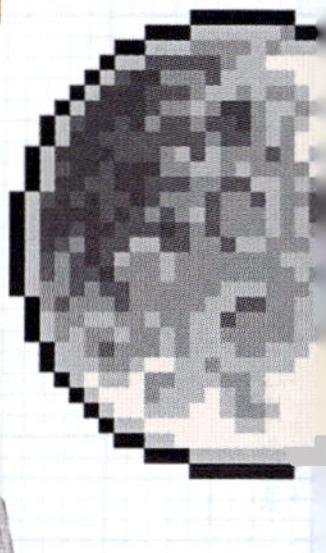

Charlie Isham and Dhara Patel

ASK AN ASTRONAUT

Meet astronaut Meganne Christian, a member of the European Space Agency astronaut reserve. This means she is a fully trained astronaut who is waiting to be called for her first mission into space!

What inspired you to become an astronaut?

When I was at school, I was absolutely fascinated by stars and planets and black holes – but it didn't actually cross my mind that it could be a career path for me! So I studied engineering, and I worked in research and material science. But it wasn't until I spent a year in Antarctica that I decided I wanted to become an astronaut. I was at the Concordia Station research base, which is also known as 'White Mars' because it's the closest thing we have on Earth to what it would be like on Mars. I was inspired by the incredible, extreme environment, and I was also really enjoying taking care of other people's experiments, which is exactly what astronauts do on the International Space Station. It seemed like the next big step would be to try and do that in space!

What is your favourite thing about training to be an astronaut?

Being underwater! It's the best way to train for spacewalks, using the buoyancy of the water to simulate weightlessness. We have a mock-up of the Columbus module (the European module on the ISS) in a pool, and we have helmets with long cords that supply air from the surface. Training as if you're on the outside of the space station was really exciting!

What science or experiments would you most look forward to doing in space?

It's really hard to choose one... so I'll choose two! One of those is 3D bioprinting. We've already tested 3D printing human tissue in space and one day we're hoping to be able to print human organs – so that instead of having to wait for a transplant from another human being on Earth, you'll actually be able to print the organs in space. The other one comes from my background as a material scientist. I spent many years working on a material called graphene, and I think you could make a purer form of it in microgravity, so I'd like to try!

What advice would you give to someone who dreams of becoming an astronaut?

I think the important thing is doing something you love, and that doesn't have to be related to space to start with. Find your passion and follow it, but know that you can change your mind along the way. That's what happened to me, because I didn't originally think of becoming an astronaut – I did lots of different things, and I was brave enough to take opportunities when they came up. There are lots of different ways of getting there!

Do you want to be an astronaut? Start your mission here >>

CONTENTS

Mission Log:
[BEGIN YOUR TRAINING]

Congratulations! You have been selected for the astronaut training programme. You will now undergo training and, if successful, you will be chosen for future missions to the International Space Station (ISS) and possibly beyond!

In your pre-flight training, you will find out about...

> Astronaut jobs
> What to wear
> Communication and controls
> Physical training
> Medical checks
> Mission Control
> Packing for space
> Survival training

WHAT SORT OF ASTRONAUT ARE YOU?

Astronauts may have many different jobs in space. When you're part of a small team, it can be important to have lots of skills. Have a look at these roles – would you rather be a pilot, a mission specialist, a payload specialist, a teacher, a spacewalker, or even all of them?

Commander/Pilot

Responsible for the mission's success, including the spacecraft's flight and overall safety. They typically have military test pilot backgrounds.

Previous experience – leadership responsibilities, STEM degree, previous flight experience

Skills – good communicator, calm under pressure, leadership skills

Eileen Collins > first woman to pilot and command the Space Shuttle

Mission Specialist

Jessica Watkins > first Black woman to live and work on the ISS for 6 months

Conducts experiments, repairs and operates spacecraft systems in space. Also performs spacewalks, operates robotics and releases small satellites.

Previous experience – scientist, engineer, doctor, or technician developing science instruments

Skills – good with computers and technology, problem-solving skills, attention to detail

Payload Specialist

Trained by private companies or research groups to operate specific equipment or carry out special experiments on space missions.

Previous experience – STEM degree, experience working in industry or research

Skills – able to use complicated equipment, good at fiddly tasks, attention to detail, great coordination

Charles Walker > first astronaut to be employed and trained by a private company to go to space

Teacher

Barbara Morgan > first teacher in space on the Space Shuttle Endeavour

Fully trained mission specialists who perform the same duties as other astronauts, while also educating students about space exploration.

Previous experience – teaching qualification and experience teaching students STEM subjects

Skills – communication skills, understands school curriculum, enjoys public speaking

Spacewalk Specialist

Performs Extravehicular Activities (EVAs), which means working outside of a spacecraft while it's in orbit.

Previous experience – STEM degree, pilot experience

Skills – calm under pressure, good coordination skills, teamwork

Cai Xuzhe (left) and Song Lingdong (right) > both hold the record for the longest EVA in a single spacewalk, at 9 hours and 6 minutes

WHERE WILL YOU GO?

If your training is successful, you will be heading to the International Space Station – but where is the ISS? How far away is it from Earth? And what will it take to get there?

Fact File: ISS

- Distance from Earth = 400 km
- Size = 109 m long (about the length of a football pitch)
- Type of object = artificial satellite
- Total number of visitors = approximately 300 people
- Orbits the Earth

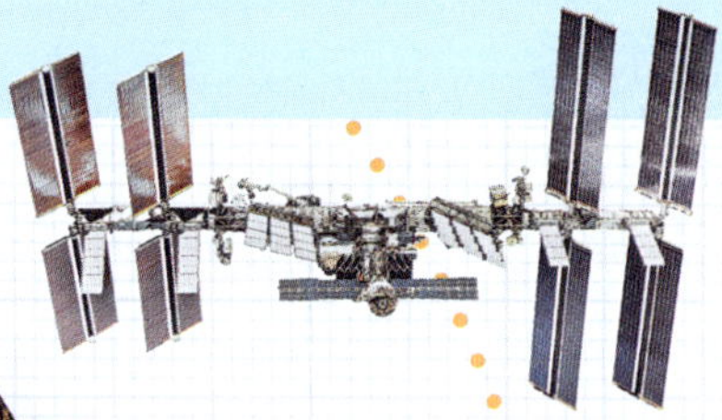

Fact File: Earth

- Size = 12,756 km in diameter
- Type of object = planet
- Inhabitants = over 8.2 billion people
- Orbits the Sun

The Kármán line

There is an agreed imaginary line around the Earth's centre, known as the equator. In a similar way, there is an accepted boundary about 100 kilometres above Earth's surface, where Earth ends and space begins. This is called the Kármán line. It might not seem very far away, but it takes huge amounts of effort and fuel to pass this boundary and reach space in a rocket.

How far away is the ISS?

To get to the ISS, you need to reach a height about four times higher than the Kármán line, around 400 kilometres above the Earth's surface. Typically, it's possible to travel to the ISS in six hours, but to conserve fuel, and depending on the timing of launch, it can take two to three days. The ISS is orbiting Earth every 90 minutes, so a rocket needs to launch at just the right time to be able to meet with the ISS.

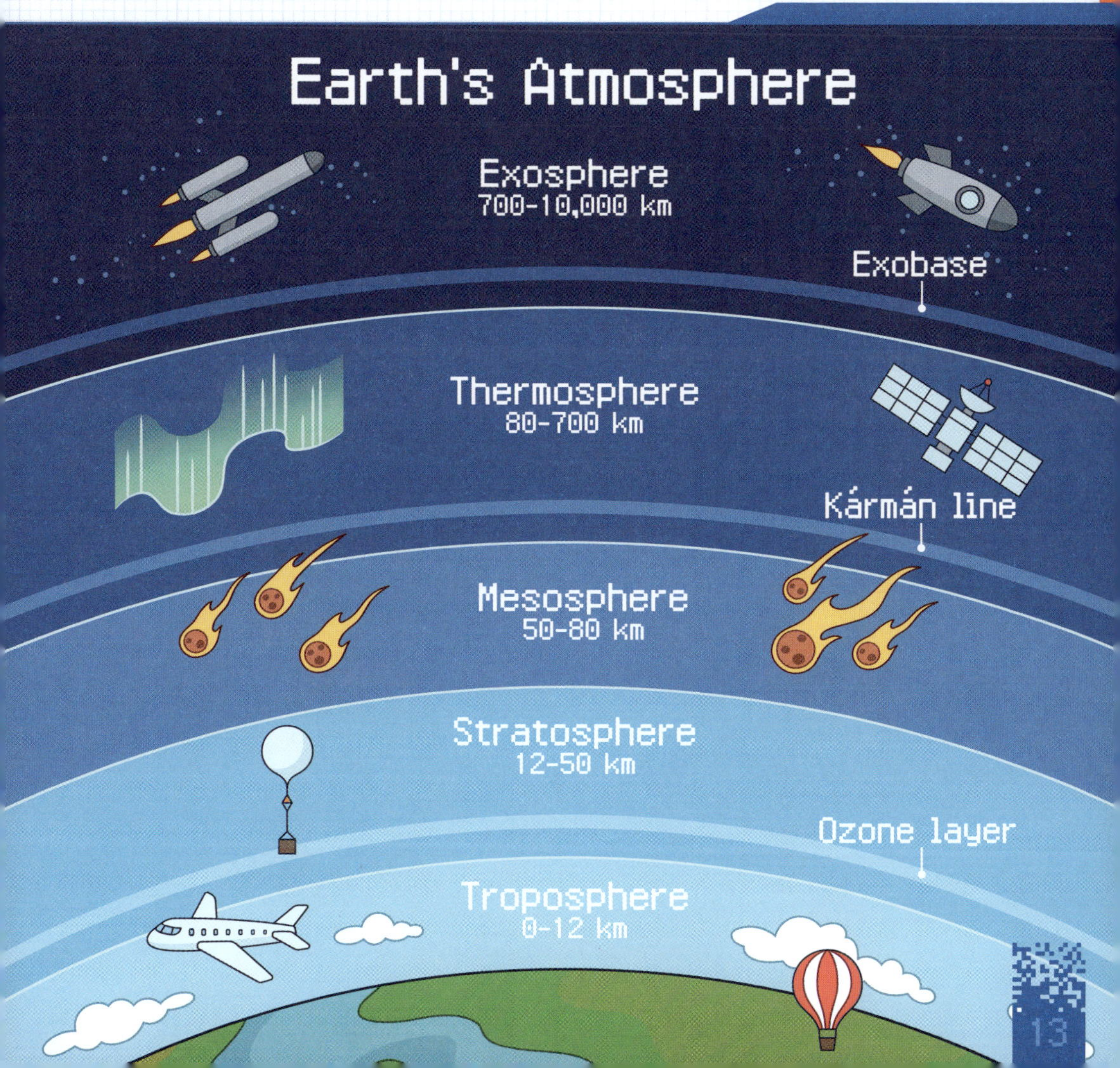

Training:

WHAT TO WEAR

Before you start basic training, you need to have the right clothing. Trainee astronauts and astronauts taking part in events normally wear a flight suit/overalls – like the one Tim Peake is wearing here. It is traditionally dark blue and has pockets and Velcro® cuffs. It is designed to be comfortable to wear for all sorts of activities.

1 Mission patch

This is a small woven patch designed to represent a specific mission or journey to space. It typically includes an image designed to show what the mission is all about.

2 Country flag

The flag of the astronaut's country is traditionally worn above the pocket on the left sleeve. For Tim, it's the Union Jack.

3 Name patch

On the left breast pocket, the flight suit will normally have a patch with the astronaut's name and an indication of their role. For example, the wings on Tim's badge tell you that he is a pilot and that he flew with the Army Air Corps.

4 Space agency patch

On the opposite side is a patch showing which space agency the astronaut is flying with. In this case, it's ESA (European Space Agency). If Tim had flown with NASA (National Aeronautics and Space Administration), it would be a NASA patch.

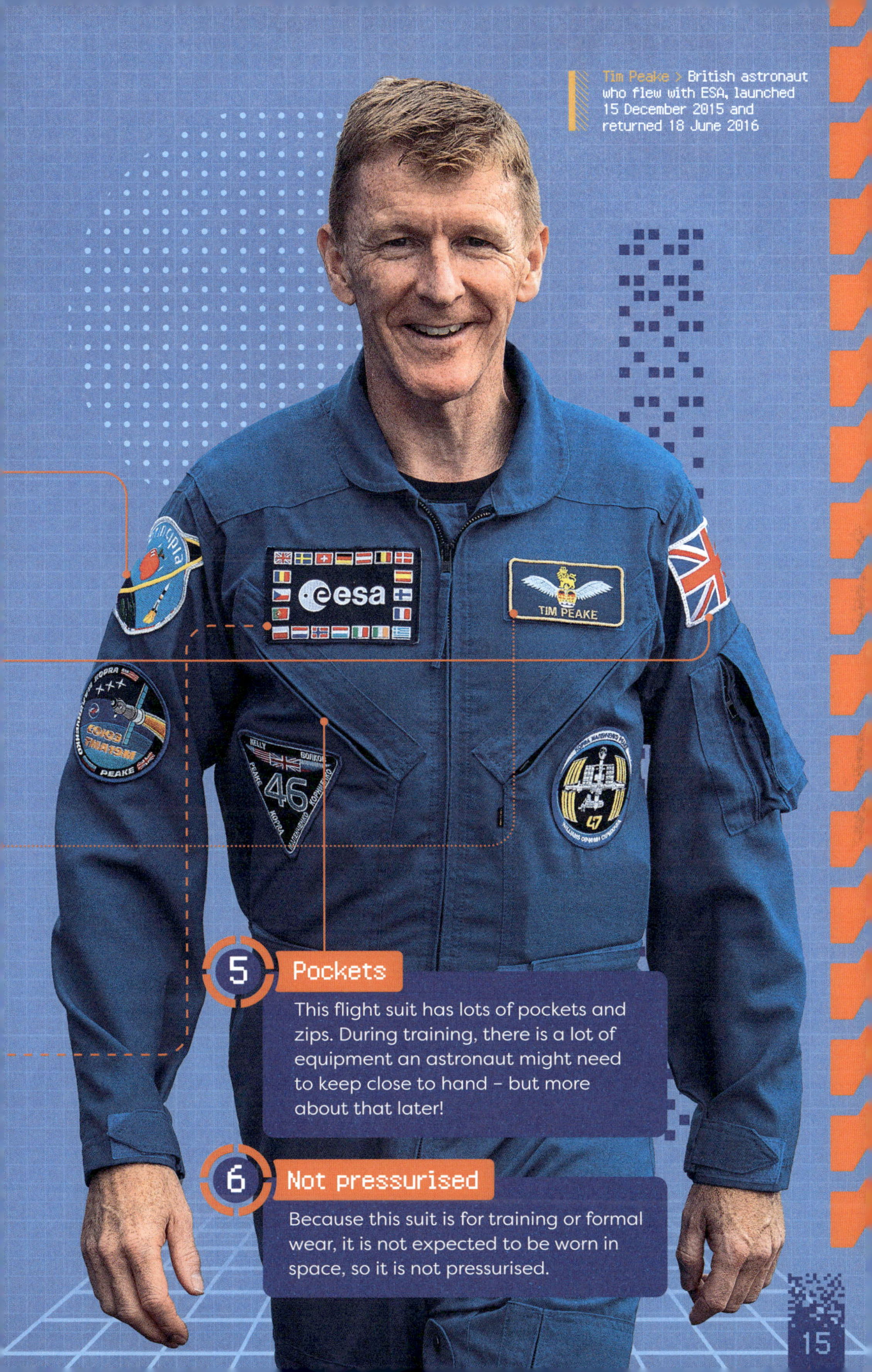

Tim Peake > British astronaut who flew with ESA, launched 15 December 2015 and returned 18 June 2016

5 Pockets

This flight suit has lots of pockets and zips. During training, there is a lot of equipment an astronaut might need to keep close to hand – but more about that later!

6 Not pressurised

Because this suit is for training or formal wear, it is not expected to be worn in space, so it is not pressurised.

Flying:

WHAT TO WEAR

For flight training, you will have to wear a high-altitude flight suit like this one. Training is likely to involve flying a jet into the upper atmosphere to practise performing tasks under pressure, even if you've never trained as a pilot. You'll also work through some of the extreme conditions astronauts experience during launch and landing.

1 Inner layer

The inner layer is a mechanical pressure suit, which is a skin-tight onesie. It's tightened using laces to create pressure on the body for when the air pressure drops on high-altitude flights (where the air is much thinner).

2 Outer layer

The topmost layer of the suit is made of a flame-resistant material. It is usually brightly coloured to make the astronaut easy to spot in an emergency.

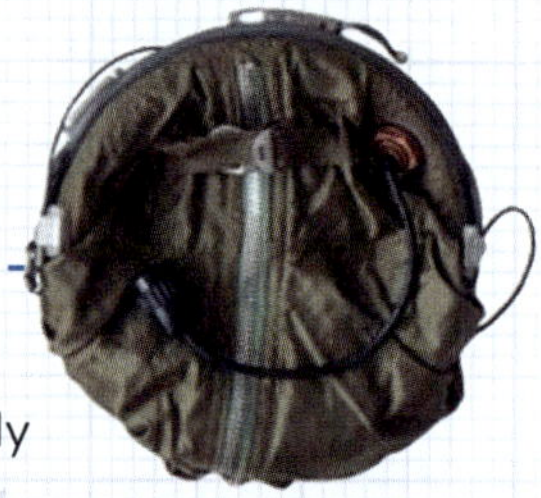

3 Air bladder

The air bladder layer fits between the inner and outer layers of the suit and covers the entire body up to the neck, wrists and ankles. It is made of rubber to make sure it is flexible and is filled with air to provide additional pressure on the body.

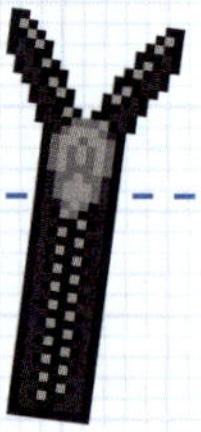

4 Zipped pockets

These provide convenient and secure storage for essential items like pens, checklists and survival gear. Zips prevent the items being lost in flight.

5 Partially pressurised

This suit is designed to be worn by pilots flying at high altitude where the air is thinner, so it is partly inflated or pressurised – but it needs to be attached to the aircraft systems to remain inflated.

VMSK-4 Soviet partial pressure suit > for pilot training at high altitude

6 Gloves, helmet, boots

You need to wear gloves, a helmet and boots during flight training. These do not provide an airtight seal with the rest of the suit.

COMMUNICATION AND CONTROLS

It's time to make sure you are prepared to face the challenges of space before your journey. Would you be able to learn the following skills?

Instructions and controls

In space, there are lots of controls to manage and instructions to follow, so it is important to make sure you know how everything works. You need to know which buttons control which parts of the spacecraft. The SpaceX Dragon capsule uses touch screen controls, which will help you to fly the spacecraft and dock with the ISS.

Learning a new language

Astronauts from lots of different countries have visited the ISS, so it is important to speak another language. Some of your crewmates might be Russian, as they fly teams of astronauts (cosmonauts) to space each year. Here are a few Russian words and phrases to help you get started.

Hello

привет **Privet** (pree-vyet)

Thank you

Спасибо **Spasibo** (spa-see-ba)

Goodbye

До свидания **Do svidaniya** (das-vee-dah-nee-yeh)

Blast-off

взлетать **vzletat** (vz-le-tat)

Managing stress on the ISS

While in space, you will need to keep your body healthy, but it is also important to look after your mental health. The ISS is a small environment with only a few people on board, and has a lot going on. This means it is important to have good teamwork skills, be resilient in difficult situations that might arise, and make decisions in stressful circumstances.

Will you stay calm in space?

PHYSICAL TRAINING

Now you've got to grips with some of the core communication and safety requirements, it's time to undergo some physical training. From launching to space to doing spacewalks, your body will be pushed to its limits. So you need to practise and prepare here on Earth for the challenges that await. Are you ready?

Underwater training

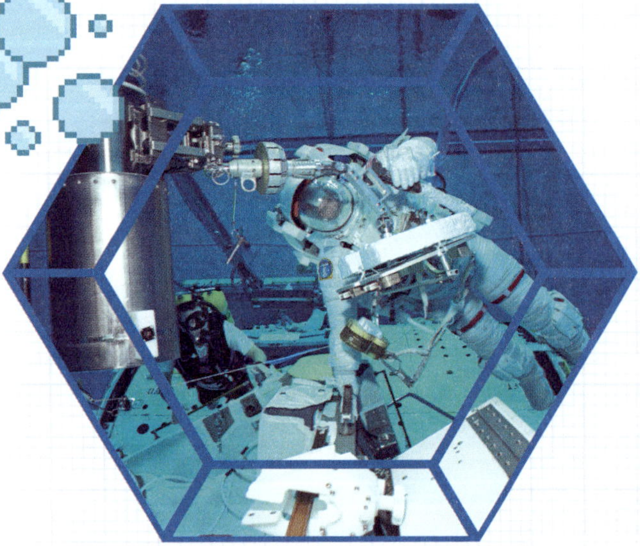

Moving around in space can be tricky. In the microgravity environment, where you feel weightless, people and objects move differently. To get you ready, you'll train in a neutral buoyancy lab, which is an underwater facility that closely mimics what it feels like in space. Here, you'll practise doing spacewalks in a bulky spacesuit, building muscle memory and coordination to prepare you for your mission.

Centrifuge

Launch and landing can put you through intense G-forces, where your body feels much heavier. This pushes you back into your seat with immense pressure. On a rollercoaster you might experience high G-forces for a few seconds, but on a space mission, they can last a few minutes! To prepare your body for the extreme forces, you'll train in a centrifuge – a device that spins you around at high speeds. Imagine that force pushing you back into your seat whilst you try to perform tasks like operating controls or lifting your arms!

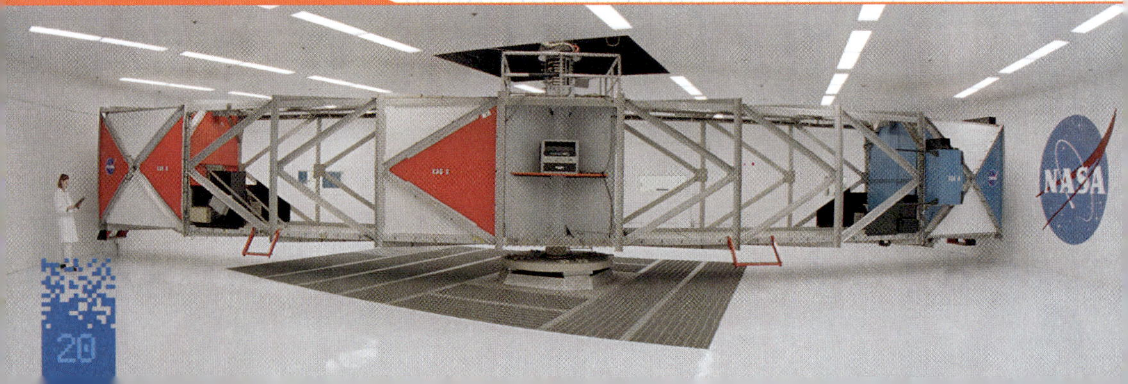

Vomit Comet

You also need to practise moving and performing tasks in microgravity. To help with this, a specially adapted plane climbs steeply into the sky. The pilot cuts the thrust and the plane pitches down headfirst, which gives you and your fellow trainees on board about half a minute of weightlessness. Our bodies aren't used to microgravity, so this experience can make you feel sick, which is why the aircraft is called the 'Vomit Comet'. Fingers crossed you manage to keep your lunch inside!

Oxygen test

If there's a leak in your spacecraft, the lowering levels of oxygen will lead to a condition called hypoxia, which can cause shortness of breath, confusion and fast breathing. As part of your training, you'll be asked to do some mental maths whilst a team carefully reduces your available oxygen. This teaches you how to recognise the symptoms of hypoxia in yourself and your crewmates, which can be lifesaving!

MINI MEDICAL

As part of your training, you'll need to complete different tests to show you are fit enough for a mission to space. You don't need to be super fit, but you do need to have a good level of fitness and be free from illness.

Eye tests

Working in space requires great eyesight, so that you can clearly see all the technical parts of the spacecraft. This doesn't mean that you can't wear glasses or contact lenses, but you must have full vision when wearing them. You will also need to take a colour blindness test, as lots of the controls on a spacecraft are colour coded. Depending on the severity of your colour blindness, it's still possible to become an astronaut – but there are certain jobs that you may not be able to do, like being a pilot.

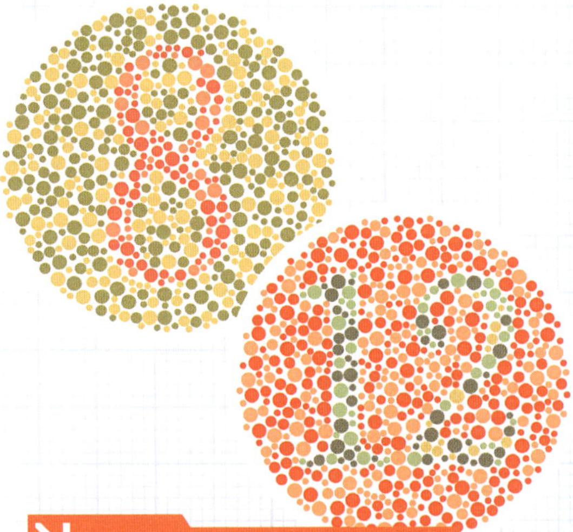

What numbers can you see in the circles?

Hearing tests

The ISS can be a very noisy place to live and work, so you need to have good hearing to be able to hear communications above the background noise. This may not be the case in the future, but for current missions this is an important part of the medical. You need to be able to hear sounds as quiet as 25 decibels. This is like the sound of quiet whispering or leaves rustling in the wind.

Height

To meet ESA regulations, you will need to be between 150 and 190 cm tall to be assigned to a space mission. This is due to the size of the spacecraft you will be travelling in. They are normally quite limited in size, so being too tall could make it difficult to fit. However, not being tall enough will make it difficult to reach the controls and equipment on the spacecraft or space station.

Blood pressure

Blood pressure measures how hard the heart is pumping to move blood around the body. NASA says that blood pressure for an astronaut should be no more than 140/90.

140 = Pressure when the heart pumps

90 = Pressure when the heart rests

Heart rate

Your heart rate is the number of times your heart beats per minute. You may be asked to do the treadmill test, which monitors your heart rate as the incline on the treadmill slowly increases. It is important for you to have a healthy heart, so that you are able to adapt to a weightless environment and cope with the physical demands of being in space.

Physical disability

In 2021, ESA put out a recruitment campaign for astronauts, but this time with a difference. They were looking for people with a physical disability to take part in a study, to see if it were feasible for them to go on a mission to space. In November 2022, British surgeon and Paralympian John McFall was selected to take part. He successfully completed the feasibility study and continues training, as he awaits a future opportunity to fly to space!

John McFall > competing in the 2008 Paralympic Games (left) and posing for his official ESA portrait in 2022 (right)

MISSION CONTROL

People in various roles will support you through your training – a space mission truly is a team effort! To manage everything between launch and landing, a ground-based command centre known as Mission Control has experts working around the clock. With help from background teams, they will keep you safe, well and on track for success.

Flight Controllers:

Experts who check specific systems like life support, flight paths, navigation, the mission schedule and your daily tasks.

CAPCOM (Capsule Communicator):

The person who communicates with you and the other astronauts in space; usually an astronaut themselves.

Flight Director:

The mission's leader who is responsible for overall safety and success. They have to make important decisions in the moment and coordinate all the different teams.

Spacecraft Operations Engineers:

Technical specialists for specific parts or instruments on the spacecraft. They check everything is operating well and work with controllers to improve things if necessary.

Flight Surgeon:

They are in charge of all medical activities during the mission. They monitor the astronauts' health from Earth.

PACKING FOR SPACE

You won't need to pack the essentials like clothes and food, as these will all be provided by the space agency. However, you will need to pack your own personal items. Your mission could take a couple of weeks, or even months. However long it is, you will only have a small bag and a maximum weight of 1.5 kg. That's less than the weight of two bags of sugar!

Things you could take to space:

- Photos of family, friends and pets
- Flags of your country
- Mission patches
- Musical instruments
- Toiletries, like toothpaste, deodorant, wet wipes
- Books

What will you pack for your trip?

Deck the ISS

At Christmas, the astronauts decorate the ISS with a tree, and new decorations are added each year.

Making music

Canadian Commander Chris Hadfield played 'Space Oddity' by David Bowie on his guitar whilst on the ISS.

Slime in space

In 2019, bright green slime was taken to space to test how it would react. It was used to teach students about different states of matter.

Making models

Japanese flight engineer Satoshi Furukawa built a model of the ISS out of plastic bricks while he was actually on board in 2011.

SURVIVAL TRAINING

Survival training gives you the best chance of dealing with unexpected challenges, like an emergency landing on Earth. As part of your training, you'll be taken to a remote and harsh environment with some basic items and equipment. Your task is to work with your fellow trainees and use the skills taught by your instructors to stay alive!

Key survival skills:

Make shelter – keep dry and warm/cool, depending on your surroundings

Find food and water – forage, build traps and snares, make fishing hooks

Navigate – use a compass or natural landmarks and stars to find your way

Stay healthy – provide first aid if needed

Await rescue – use inflatables to stay afloat in the sea

Survival kit

Every spacecraft is packed with a survival kit containing useful equipment in case of landing in the wilderness – like this Russian survival kit that was used by pilots and cosmonauts from the late 1960s onwards.

Here are some of the basic items astronauts may have in their survival kits.

1. **Water/desalter kits**
These give you an immediate source of drinking water or the ability to purify it.

2. **Firestarter and waterproof matches**
These help you light a fire, to keep warm or cook food.

3. **First-aid box**
This includes medical dressings for injuries, as well as medicines with instructions on how to use them.

4. **Signal flares**
Distress flares attract attention and let rescuers know you're in need of help.

5. **Food rations**
These are concentrated sources of energy, like caramel, for a quick energy boost during a crisis.

6. **Radio**
You can use emergency radio frequencies to broadcast your location and listen for instructions.

7. **Mirror**
A mirror reflects sunlight and lets you signal for help to aircraft flying above.

8. **Knives**
These are for food preparation, setting up camp, building things, etc.

9. **Protective gear**
Items like sunglasses and blankets protect you in different environments.

10. **Parachute silk**
This is lightweight material that can be used for shelter.

DIY Space Experiment:
ASTRONAUT CHALLENGE

The following three tasks will test your:

- **Dexterity** – how easily you can handle objects skillfully
- **Coordination** – how different parts of your body work together
- **Cognition** – how you think and figure things out
- **Reaction time** – how quickly you can respond

Dexterity test

On a spacewalk, you will wear a spacesuit made of many different layers, which will make it tricky to do tasks with your hands. This dexterity test will help you practise handling objects as if you are wearing your spacesuit.

What you need:

- Three different-sized pairs of gloves
- A jigsaw

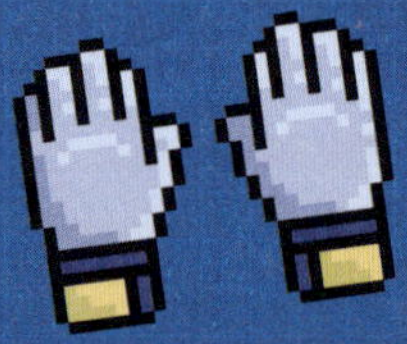

What to do:

First, have a go at completing a jigsaw. Then put on three different-sized gloves (one on top of the other) and try completing the jigsaw again with the gloves on. You could time yourself and see how quickly you can do it.

Do you think you could work in a spacesuit?

Coordination and cognition test

When you are an astronaut, you sometimes have to communicate information whilst also coordinating your body in space.

What you need:

- A friend or family member
- A step

What to do:

In this test, get a friend or family member to read the 'forwards' numbers from the table, then have a go at repeating them backwards. What's the longest chain of numbers you can remember?

Now try stepping on and off a step whilst repeating the numbers backwards to see how good your coordination is. Was it more challenging doing both tasks together?

Forwards	*Backwards*
897	798
036	630
951	159
6978	8796
4910	0194
3182	2813
57806	60875
42319	91324
513728	827315
5749681	1869475
4609375	5739064
94815302	20351849
956180427	724081659
0389561427	7241659830
7923518640	0468153297
451769382025	520283967154

How would you react under pressure in space?

Reaction time test

Space can be a dangerous place, and you need to be able to react quickly to deal with emergency situations.

What you need:

- A friend or family member
- A ruler

What to do:

Get your friend or a family member to hold a ruler vertically in the air with zero at the bottom. Place your hand in a c-shape at the bottom of the ruler, ready to catch it. Without telling you, they should drop the ruler, and you need to catch it as quickly as possible. Have a look at the distance on the ruler at the top of your thumb, then use the table to work out your reaction time. How quickly were you able to react?

Distance (cm)	Reaction time (milliseconds)
1	50
2	60
3	70
4	80
5	90
6	100
7	120
8	130
9	140
10	140
11	150
12	160
13	160
14	170
15	170
16	180
17	190
18	190
19	200
20	200
21	210
22	210
23	220
24	220
25	230
26	230
27	230
28	240
29	240
30	250

Reaction time (milliseconds)	Rating
0–80	Ultra-fast
81–130	Excellent
131–175	Good
176–200	Average
201–240	Fair
241–250	Slow

NASA
NASA
ARTEMIS

Mission Log:
[KNOW YOUR ROCKET]

Well done, recruit! You have successfully completed your astronaut training. Before you are assigned to your first space mission, you'll need to know more about rockets and how they work.

Continue reading for further instructions on...

> The history of rockets
> What's inside a rocket?
> Fuels and blasting off
> Spaceports around the world
> Getting to the ISS
> New ways to travel

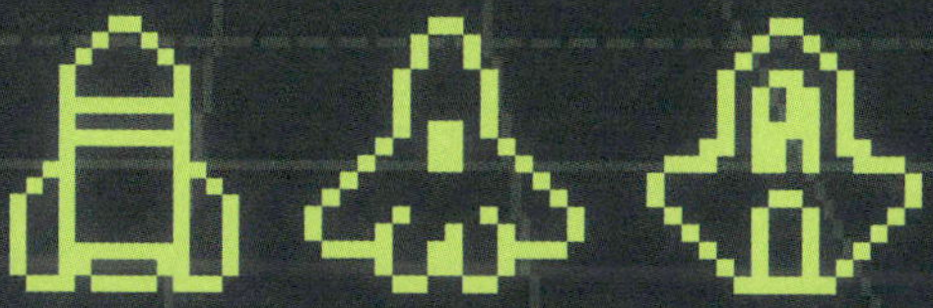

HISTORY OF ROCKETS

Rockets have been around in some form or another for hundreds of years. This timeline shows some of the major developments in rocket technology, and the type of rocket you might be working in during your space missions!

1 **1232**
Gunpowder-filled bamboo tubes were used in battle by the Chinese.

2 **1926**
Robert Goddard launched the first liquid-fuelled rocket.

3 **1944**
The V2 was the first human-made object to reach space. It was launched from Germany.

4 **1957**
The Soviet Union launched the first satellite, called Sputnik 1.

5 **1961**
Yuri Gagarin from the Soviet Union became the first human to go into space. He was launched into orbit in a Vostok rocket.

6 1966

The first Soyuz rocket launched from Kazakhstan. It has become one of the most reliable and frequently used human spaceflight rocket systems.

7 1967

The first Saturn V rocket was launched from Florida, USA. In 1969, it became the first type of rocket to launch astronauts to the Moon.

8 1979

The first Ariane 1 rocket was launched from French Guiana by ESA.

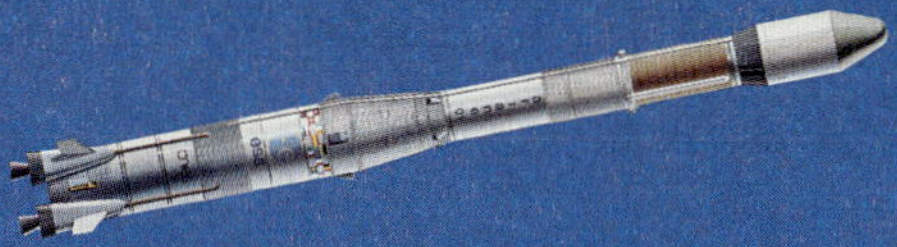

9 1981

NASA launched its first space shuttle mission in the Space Transportation System (STS-1) Program from Florida. Space Shuttle Columbia, the world's first re-usable spacecraft, had a huge area for transporting astronauts and equipment.

10 2026

As part of NASA's Artemis Program, the Space Launch System (SLS) rocket launched from Florida for its test flight in 2022. More recently, the SLS took a crew of four astronauts on a 10-day trip around the Moon in 2026 on the Artemis II mission – paving the way for astronauts like you to travel to the lunar surface and to other destinations like Mars in the future.

WHAT'S INSIDE A ROCKET?

Before you go into space, it's important to get to know how a rocket works. You'll be strapped into your spacecraft, which will sit at the top of the rocket. It's useful to understand its different parts and what happens in each area of the rocket.

1 Cargo area

The top of the rocket, in the nose cone, is where the cargo area is. This is where equipment, spacecraft or astronauts like you will travel to space.

2 Guidance system

Still within the nose cone but underneath the cargo area is the guidance system, which includes computers and communication equipment to support the rocket when it is in flight.

3 Fuel

The huge amounts of fuel needed to get the rocket to launch are stored in large tanks (liquid hydrogen and liquid oxygen).

4 Solid Rocket Boosters

On each side of the rocket, you might see Solid Rocket Boosters (or SRBs). There are usually between two and six SRBs, but some rockets have none at all.

5 Exhaust nozzle

At the bottom of the rocket is the exhaust nozzle, which squeezes exhaust gases from the engine. From here, huge amounts of burning gases are expelled at high speed from the rocket.

ESA's Ariane 5 rocket >
Standing tall at around 53 metres, it flew 117 times between 1996 and 2023, launching satellites and spacecraft into space

FUELS AND BLASTING OFF

Blast off, when a rocket lifts off the launch pad and begins its journey into space, is an exciting moment for an astronaut, and for Mission Control. But how does a rocket manage to launch?

How are rockets fuelled?

Most rockets today use combustion engines, fuelled by liquid fuels – usually liquid oxygen mixed with either liquid hydrogen or kerosene. Some rockets also use solid fuel in the form of Solid Rocket Boosters.

What is a combustion engine?

A rocket combustion engine works by burning liquid fuels continuously, creating extremely hot gases up to 3,000°C. These hot gases are forced at high speeds through the nozzle, a bit like a car exhaust. This gives the rocket the push, or thrust, it needs to move forwards, in the opposite direction, away from Earth.

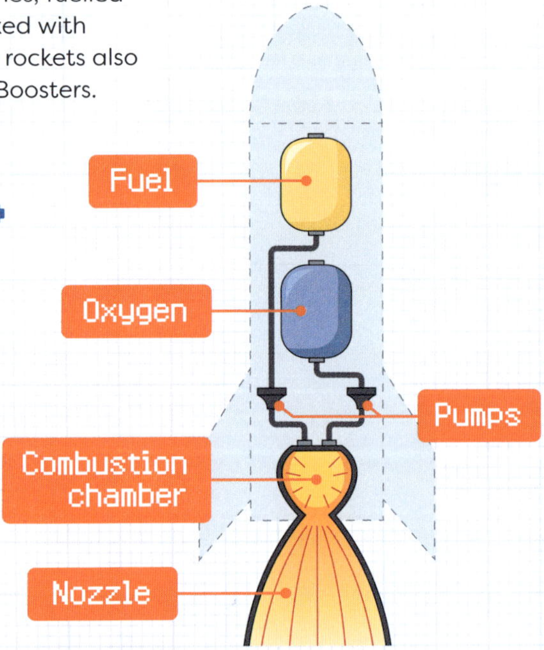

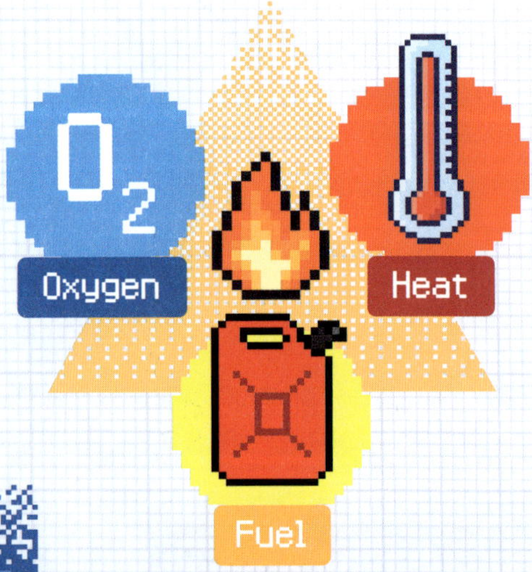

The fire triangle

Combustion is another way of saying burning, and that's exactly what these engines do. They burn fuels to create the hot gases needed for launch. However, to be able to burn something you need three things: fuel, heat and oxygen. This is sometimes known as the fire triangle – when you take one item away, the fire will start to go out. As there isn't a steady supply of oxygen in space, rockets take their own liquid oxygen to help burn their fuel.

SRBs

Solid Rocket Boosters are used by many rockets, such as the Space Launch System (SLS) and Ariane 5 rocket, in the first stages of launch. They contain solid fuel and normally provide the bulk of the thrust needed for launch. Nearly two-thirds of the energy needed for launch can come from SRBs, which help to overcome Earth's pull of gravity.

NASA's SLS rocket uses two huge SRBs, each the size of a 17-storey building, for just 126 seconds. Each booster generates more thrust than 14 four-engine jumbo commercial aeroplanes.

Newton's third law

All rockets work using basic principles from physics, the main one being Newton's third law: for every action, there is an equal and opposite reaction. For a rocket, this means that the hot burning gases being forced out of one end of the rocket push the rocket in the opposite direction, away from Earth.

You can try out Newton's third law at home with a balloon. Blow up the balloon and let it go without tying it. How does it move? You'll notice that the air rushes out and makes the balloon fly away. This is similar to what happens when a rocket launches.

SPACEPORTS AROUND THE WORLD

You've got to grips with how rockets work, but where do they launch from? When you travel from one country to another, you often use an airport. In a similar way, spaceports are places where rockets and other spacecraft are launched from Earth to space. Many spaceports only launch robotic spacecraft (spacecraft without people on board). Only a few are able to launch humans into orbit: Cape Canaveral, Kennedy, Jiuquan and Baikonur.

Lots of room

Spaceports don't just include the launch pad – they control huge areas of surrounding land for safety reasons, in case a rocket has to be destroyed in flight.

Middle of nowhere

Launches are explosive and powerful events, so spaceports are usually built far from populated areas, or close to the sea, for example in deserts or by the coast. This is to minimise the risk of damage to communities, or injuries to humans.

Prime location

Many spaceports are located near the equator. This is because as a rocket launches it can use the spin of the Earth, which is fastest at the equator, to boost its speed. This means that it needs less fuel to reach the 28,000 kilometres per hour required to get into orbit!

The world's biggest

Baikonur in Kazakhstan is the world's first and largest operational spaceport. It covers over 6,500 square kilometres – that's more than four times the size of Greater London!

GETTING TO THE ISS

Different countries use different rockets and spacecraft to launch astronauts to the ISS. In 2000, a Russian Soyuz rocket with two cosmonauts and one astronaut on board lifted off from Baikonur. The arrival of this first crew marked the start of the ISS being continuously crewed. Since then, over 300 people have lived and worked there – are you ready to join this exclusive group of space explorers?

The nose cone – carries the crew and cargo.

Upper liquid-fuelled segment – to help get the rocket into orbit.

Central liquid-fuelled core – to help the rocket reach space.

Four liquid-fuelled strap-on boosters – to help with blasting off!

Soyuz TMA-9 spacecraft > launching from Baikonur

New and improved

A modernised version of the Soyuz rocket is still used today to launch astronauts to the ISS. Between 2011 and 2020, this was the only way to travel to and from the ISS. The Soyuz spacecraft at the National Space Centre is an example of the crew-carrying spacecraft that would sit at the top of a Soyuz rocket!

Soyuz 7K-OK spacecraft > on display at the National Space Centre, Leicester

The Space Shuttle

Until 2011, Americans used the Space Shuttle system to transport astronauts to and from the ISS. It launched from NASA's Kennedy Space Center in Florida. The Soyuz spacecraft was not designed to be re-usable – a new one was needed for each flight. However, the Space Shuttle could return safely to Earth, so it could be re-used. It used a runway landing, and after some servicing and maintenance it launched another crew to the ISS.

Space Shuttle Discovery >
launching from Kennedy Space Center

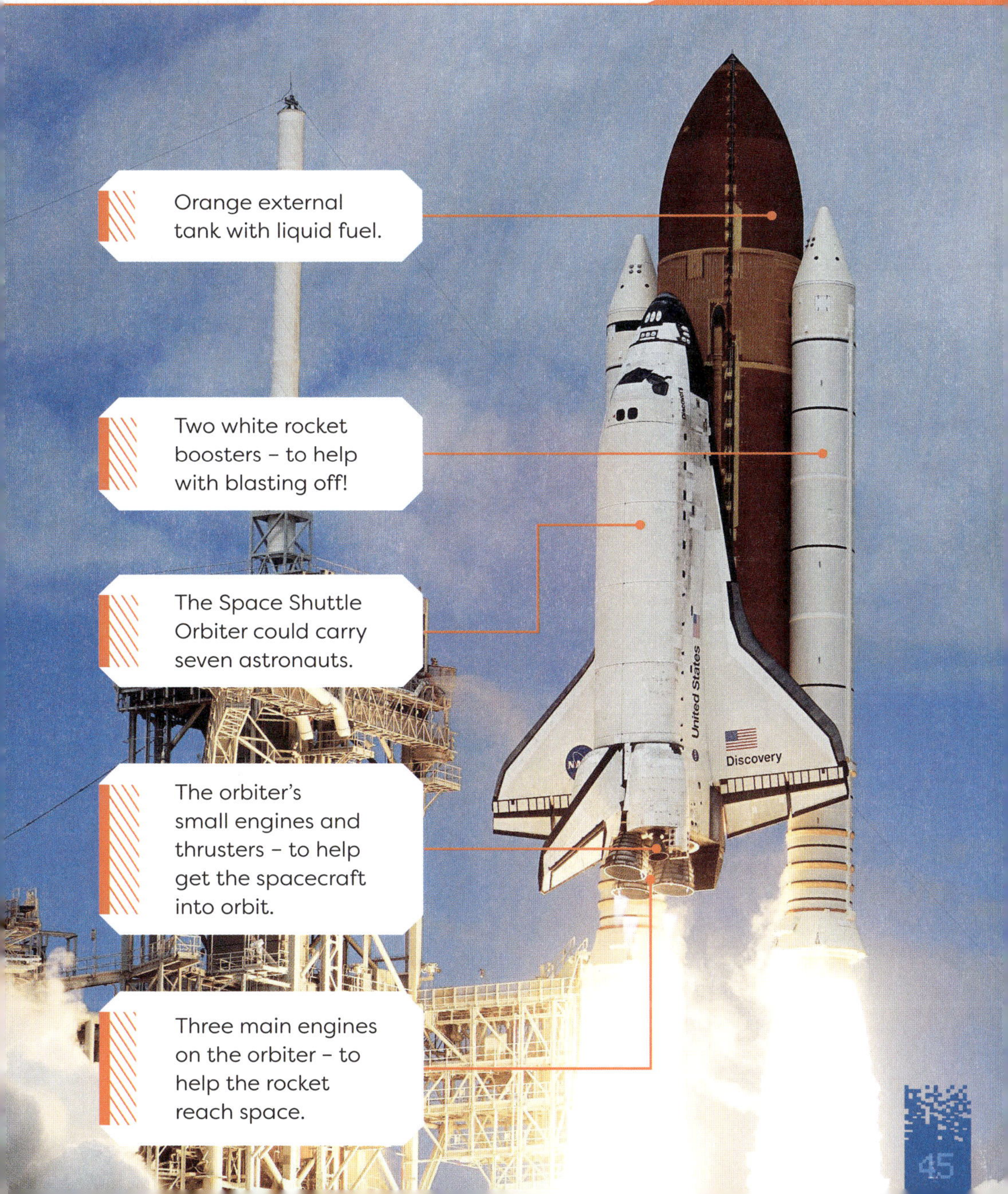

NEW WAYS TO TRAVEL

It's becoming more common for government space organisations like NASA and ESA to work with private space companies in their space endeavours. Since 2020, NASA have used the SpaceX Falcon 9 rocket to launch crews to the ISS. The SpaceX Crew Dragon capsule that sits on the top of this rocket can transport four astronauts – one of those could be you!

The SpaceX Crew Dragon capsule in the nose cone.

Single engine liquid-fuelled re-startable tank – to help the rocket reach space.

Nine-engine, liquid-fuelled re-usable tank – to help with blasting off!

After the fuel in the lift-off stage is used, the re-usable part of the rocket returns to Earth and lands upright, either in a landing facility on the ground or on a landing pad out at sea (below). It's then given a service and an MOT, like a car, before being prepared for another launch.

SpaceX Falcon 9 >
launching from Kennedy Space Center

Just Read the Instructions

SpaceX has three barges used as landing platforms for recovering rockets at sea. They are called *Of Course I Still Love You*, *Just Read the Instructions* and *A Shortfall of Gravitas*.

Exploring beyond the ISS

As humans prepare to explore further out into space, larger rockets are being built by private companies that are capable of taking people to the Moon.

SpaceX Starship

Starship is still being developed by the American company, SpaceX. The idea is that it will be fully re-usable, so both parts of the rocket will return to Earth safely. They will be caught by the arms on the launch tower, re-fuelled and prepared for the next mission.

SpaceX Starship >
standing at Starbase, Texas

New Glenn

Another American private company, Blue Origin, has developed the New Glenn rocket (named after the first American astronaut to orbit the Earth, John Glenn). This two-stage rocket is partly re-usable. The first (bottom) stage of the rocket is engineered to return to the Earth after launch and is designed to be re-used for at least 25 missions.

DIY Space Experiment:

MAKE A ROCKET REACTION

Create an exciting rocket reaction at home with simple chemicals from your kitchen!

★ ★ ★ ★ ★

What you need:

- 3 x plastic bottles (500 ml)
- 3 x balloons
- Bicarbonate of soda
- Lemon or lime juice
- Water
- Washing up liquid
- Ruler and pen
- Paper cone or funnel (optional)

What to do:

1 Mark the bottles

Mark each bottle with a horizontal line approximately 2cm from the bottom.

2 Add the liquids

Fill one bottle up to the line with washing up liquid, another with water, and the third with lemon or lime juice.

3 Fill the balloons

Put two teaspoons of bicarbonate of soda into each balloon and twist the top to keep the soda from falling out. You can use a paper cone or funnel to help with this.

4 Attach the balloons

Carefully attach the end of each balloon to the top of each of the bottles, being careful not to spill any of the soda inside the bottle.

5 Untwist the balloons

One by one, as quickly as possible, untwist and hold the balloon upright so that soda falls into the liquid in each bottle.

6 Watch the reaction

Now watch carefully as the ingredients react together. Which of your three bottles inflated the balloon the most?

What's the science?

A chemical reaction between the substances has produced carbon dioxide gas. The bubbles and pressure of the carbon dioxide inflate the balloon. Similarly, a rocket uses fuel and oxygen in a combustion reaction to produce water and carbon dioxide, and of course energy, causing it to lift off!

Mission Log:
[TIME FOR LIFT-OFF]

Congratulations, you've completed your general rocket training and you're ready for your first mission to the ISS. It's time to strap in and prepare for lift-off.

In this next stage, you'll find out about...

> Pre-flight planning
> What you'll wear for lift-off
> Spaceflight traditions
> The launch pad
> Strapping in for lift-off
> The countdown to launch
> The journey to the ISS

PRE-FLIGHT PLANNING

In the weeks and days ahead of launch, it's time for final preparations to ensure that the mission will be a success.

Launch window

Part of the pre-flight planning involves identifying a launch window – when it's most suitable to launch. This window is affected by a few different factors:

Orbital factors

A precisely timed lift-off is needed so that the spacecraft can meet with the ISS in its orbit. Just like relay racers passing a baton, if you approach at the wrong angle or the wrong speed, it may not be possible to link up.

Environmental factors

High winds, thunderstorms and unsettled conditions in the upper atmosphere may delay and cancel a launch, also known as scrubbing a launch.

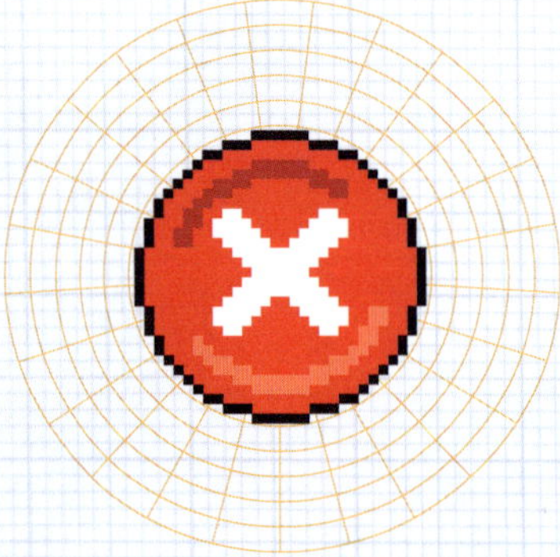

Technical factors

Sometimes technical things can alter plans. For instance, the rocket's engines might not be working as efficiently as they should – this can cause the launch path to change, which also affects the launch window.

Pre-flight timeline

Because of these factors, you've got to be ready to go, but also be flexible as plans can change at the last minute! All being well, your pre-flight timeline will look like this...

Two weeks before launch

Your health quarantine begins, and you have limited contact with people. This means living in a special confined environment with daily check-ups to ensure you're healthy and without any illnesses that you could carry into space.

You will have some mission briefings – final meetings with the crew and ground control to go over the different aspects of the mission.

During quarantine, you'll get to spend some time with your family, which may be through video calls or through glass in separate rooms, as physical contact is restricted.

Day of launch

Wake up and have breakfast.

Get into your Intravehicular Activity suit (IVA), which can take at least 45 minutes.

Have your final health checks.

Say a final (socially distanced) goodbye to your family – air hugs, waves and blowing kisses.

Travel to the launch pad in the designated transport vehicle.

Time for lift off!

Lift-off:

WHAT TO WEAR

On the day of the launch, you'll get into your spacesuit, ready for blasting off into space! You'll wear an Intravehicular Activity suit (IVA) inside the spacecraft during launch and landing. It is not designed to be used on spacewalks, because it doesn't have suitable protection against radiation, micrometeoroids (tiny space rocks) and space debris (small pieces of human-made material). You'll enter the suit through a front opening, which is sealed by a pressure-tight zipper.

1 Helmet

The helmet has a ring that seals it tightly to the neck ring, and a radio headset inside.

2 Name tag

A patch with your name (in Russian and English).

3 Valve

The valve releases air and reduces pressure inside the suit.

4 Manufacturer's patch

A patch with the logo of the company that made the suit (in this case, Zvezda).

5 Gauge

The gauge monitors pressure inside the suit.

6 Gloves

Detachable gloves twist and lock to the suit.

7 Umbilical cords

Umbilical cords are used to connect the suit to the life support system on the spacecraft, in case you need an oxygen supply and electrical power. In an emergency, if the spacecraft gets damaged and is no longer sealed, the umbilical cords will inflate the suit with pressurised air and oxygen. This will keep you in a sealed 'bubble' for a couple of hours. It should stop you from overheating and let you breathe as if you are on Earth.

Sokol KV-2 Rescue Spacesuit >
an example of an IVA suit -
fully pressurised when the
suit is inflated

8 National flag

A patch with the astronaut's national flag (in this case, the Union Jack).

9 Mirror

A mirror lets you see things outside your direct line of sight.

Invented for space

The lining of the seat that astronauts sit in contains memory foam to keep the astronaut comfortable during launch and landing. Memory foam was developed by NASA researchers but is now used in many ways on Earth, like in pillows and mattresses.

SPACEFLIGHT TRADITIONS

In the past, astronauts have done certain things in the lead-up to the launch – for example, played card games, had a final toilet stop, designed a mission patch and named their spacecraft. Over time, these have become traditions or superstitions that astronauts follow for good luck. What spaceflight tradition are you going to start?

Possum's Fargo

Before they head to the launch pad, NASA astronauts play a card game called 'Possum's Fargo' in the room they get suited up in. The Commander of the mission has to lose a game, so that any bad luck is left in the room.

Weeing on a bus wheel

When Yuri Gagarin was on the bus to the launch pad in 1961, he realised he needed to relieve himself one last time before lift-off. He stepped out of the bus and urinated on the back right tyre – a gesture that is copied by almost every Russian and international crew member going to the ISS from the Baikonur spaceport.

Gagarin's mission was a huge success and this ritual of weeing on the tyre of the transporter bus is seen as a good luck charm. Women aren't required to do so, but some bring a pot of their own urine to pour on the tyre, to honour the tradition.

Mission patch

Valentina Tereshkova was the first person to wear a mission patch in space in 1963. However, it was covered by her spacesuit. The first crew-designed and outwardly worn mission patch was worn by NASA astronauts Gordon Cooper and Pete Conrad in 1965 on their Gemini 5 mission. Since then, it has become a tradition for a crew to design a patch to symbolise and celebrate their mission. These embroidered patches are sewn on spacesuits and worn like a badge of honour!

The mission name.

Slogan '8 Days or Bust' – they were aiming to complete an 8-day spaceflight (the longest to date at that time).

Conestoga wagon – used by explorers in the 18th and 19th centuries, picked by the crew to represent their mission into the unknown.

Astronaut names.

What would you include on a patch for your space mission?

Spacecraft names

Along with mission patches, it has become a tradition to name spacecraft For example, Apollo 11 astronauts named their lunar lander 'Eagle'. This represents the national emblem of America, a bald eagle, which is known for its strength, courage and freedom. And it's why Neil Armstrong said 'The Eagle has landed' in July 1969, to share that he and Buzz Aldrin had successfully landed the spacecraft on the Moon.

Some unusual and comical names have been given to spacecraft. Apollo 9 astronauts called their lunar lander 'Spider', as the four-legged spacecraft reminded them of one.

THE LAUNCH PAD

When you arrive at the launch pad, the spacecraft at the top of the rocket will be ready for you to board. A couple of weeks before launch, the rocket is rolled out from the building it's assembled in, onto the launch pad. Sometimes that journey is tens of kilometres and the rocket is transported horizontally along a specialised rail track, like at Baikonur. Other journeys are just a few kilometres, and the rocket is transported vertically on a crawler vehicle along a road, like at Kennedy Space Center.

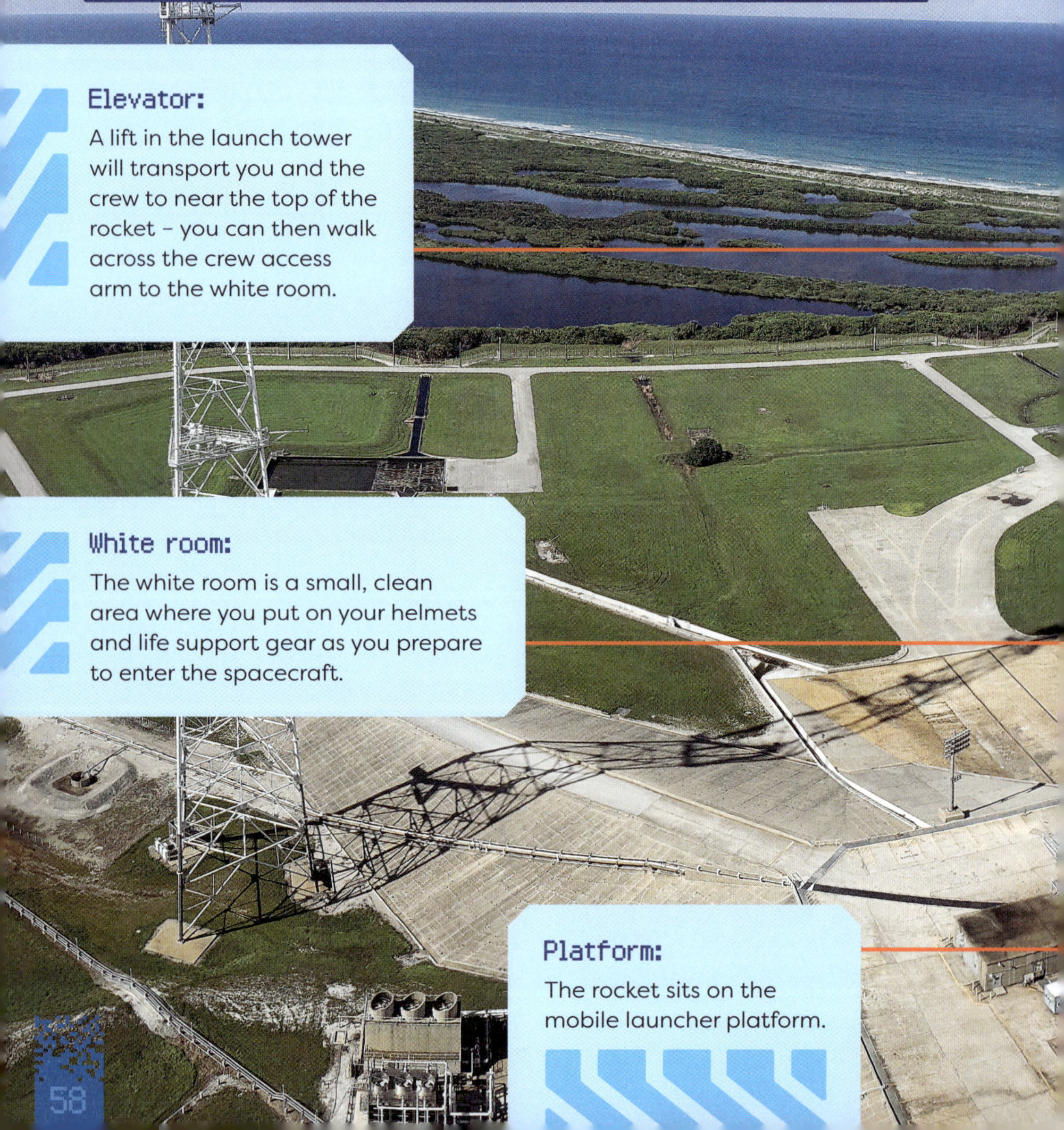

Elevator:

A lift in the launch tower will transport you and the crew to near the top of the rocket – you can then walk across the crew access arm to the white room.

White room:

The white room is a small, clean area where you put on your helmets and life support gear as you prepare to enter the spacecraft.

Platform:

The rocket sits on the mobile launcher platform.

Lightning towers:

A few tall lightning towers (taller than the rocket) provide alternative and easier paths for lightning to follow, preventing strikes on the rocket.

Cables:

Cables from the launch tower connect to the rocket and spacecraft, providing power before the launch.

Flame trench:

The flame trench (about the length of one and a half football fields) helps to guide the hot gases safely away and withstands temperatures of 1,200°C during launch!

A water tower with enough water to fill 27 swimming pools is dumped on the mobile launcher platform and in the flame trench in under 30 seconds. It helps to extinguish the powerful sounds and pressures during launch.

STRAPPING IN FOR LIFT-OFF

The launch window has arrived, you've got through quarantine, performed some good luck traditions and everything is looking nominal – that means it is all going as planned. You're wearing your IVA suit and you've travelled in the lift to the top of the launch tower. This is it – time to get strapped into the spacecraft!

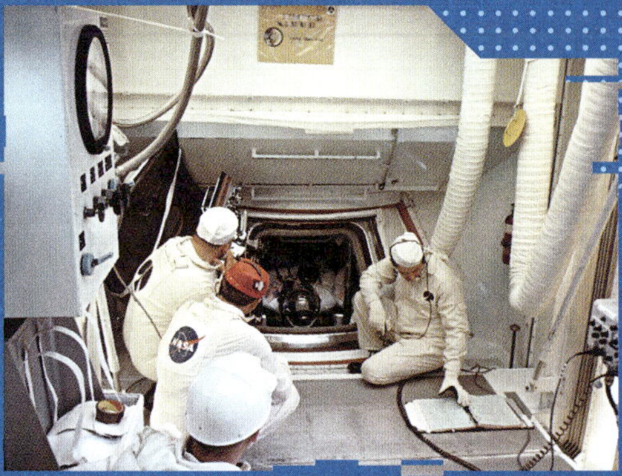

Suit and systems check

A team known as the 'closeout crew' will help you get into the spacecraft – it's a snug fit! Your suit will be checked and you'll sit hunched on your back (as during launch you are facing up towards the sky). The pressure inside the spacecraft is checked, along with communication systems, to ensure you and the rest of the crew can speak to ground control.

No more toilet breaks!

This process can take several hours as it's the final chance to perform checks. So you'll need to wear a maximum absorbency garment inside your spacesuit (like a nappy), as there's no option to use the toilet now!

Zero-G indicator

The only other 'passenger' on board is a zero-G indicator – a small, lightweight object such as a plush toy that begins to float once you reach space. This is so you can tell when you've left the strong pull of Earth's gravity and are weightless!

The hatch is closed

All buckled up, the closeout crew secures the hatch, leaving you securely inside the spacecraft. It's just you and your crew now.

Safety procedures

From within the spacecraft cabin, you and your crew will go through emergency protocols. About 37 minutes before lift-off, the launch escape system will be activated. This vital safety feature uses special rockets which start automatically or manually if a launch fails. The crew capsule is quickly pulled away to a safe distance, where its parachutes can deploy and bring everyone back to Earth.

Fuelling and power

At the same time, the rocket is also loaded with fuel. The spacecraft changes from using power provided via cable from the launch tower to its own internal batteries.

The moments before countdown

As you wait for the final countdown, you'll communicate with Mission Control to help you stay focused and calm. You can also listen to music. Soon, it'll be time to close your helmet visor and ready yourself for a rollercoaster ride of a lifetime, where you'll experience going from 0 to 28,000 kilometres per hour in just over eight minutes!

Which songs would you listen to while you wait for launch?

COUNTDOWN TO LAUNCH: 10, 9, 8...

Whilst the crew is preparing themselves inside the spacecraft, Mission Control carries out final checks to make sure everything is ready for lift-off. The countdown contains 'L-minus' and 'T-minus' times. 'L-minus' shows the time left until lift-off in hours and minutes. 'T-minus' is a sequence of events that are built into the launch countdown.

L-40 minutes:

The levels of the fuel must be checked, and liquid propellant and oxidiser (O_2) need to be filled up.

L-15 minutes:

Go or no-go – The launch director will check with each team to see if they are 'go' (ready) for launch.

T-10 minutes:

The spacecraft is changed to using internal power, rather than from the launch tower, and hydrogen burn-off igniters are fired to safely burn any extra hydrogen gas on the launch pad and prevent a dangerous blast.

T-1 minute and 30 seconds:

Up until this point, the clock can be restarted to T-10 at any time. However, if there is any need to stop the launch past T-1 minute and 30 seconds, the launch will be aborted for that day. If all is well, the rocket will then start the final countdown to launch.

T-0:

Boosters are ignited and clamps are released so that the rocket is separated from the tower.

Launch:

The Mission Control team will celebrate the successful launch of the rocket, while still carefully monitoring its progress until it reaches its destination.

JOURNEY TO THE ISS

Now the rocket has taken off, you have at least a six-hour journey before you reach the ISS. Although you're protected by the rocket and your flight suit, your body will experience high levels of vibrations, G-force and then weightlessness.

0-2 minutes

From the engine thrusters firing just before lift-off until around two minutes into launch, you will feel huge amounts of vibrations throughout your body. This shaking of the rocket also increases noise levels inside to 140 decibels – similar to the noise of a fireworks display. To protect you from these high levels of sound, you have ear protection in your flight suit. The ear plugs, communication headset and your helmet will dampen the sound significantly.

0-9 minutes

During take-off, you will feel G-force pushing you back into your seat. This can make it difficult to move and your entire body feel three or four times as heavy as it really is. You may need to use a special stick to help you press controls. This feeling lasts until the rocket reaches orbit.

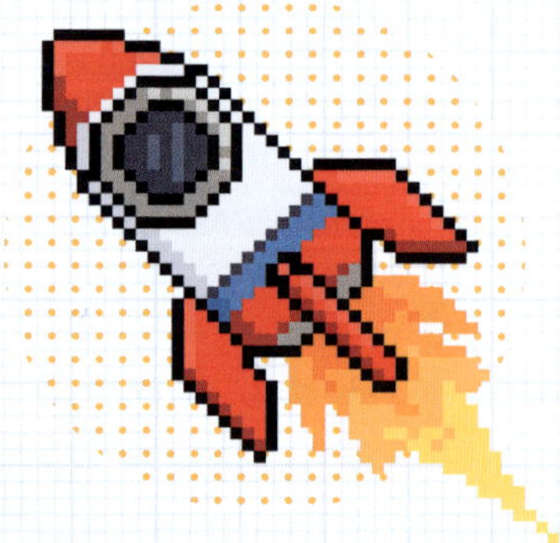

9-10 minutes onwards

At this point into the launch, the rocket reaches a speed of just over 28,000 kilometres per hour. This is the speed needed to stay in orbit around the Earth. The rocket at this point shuts down its main engines and has reached 100 kilometres above the Earth's surface. Smaller engines then take the spacecraft into the desired orbit or altitude.

The sky

As you move away from Earth's atmosphere, the blue sky outside the window will change to black. You will start to see an amazing view of the Earth, called the 'Blue Marble' by other astronauts. As you see this beautiful sight, it's time to reflect on the uniqueness of our home planet!

Feeling weightless

Once the spacecraft goes into orbit and freefall around the Earth, you will begin to feel weightless, see the zero-G indicator begin floating and you will start to float if you are not harnessed into your seat. You will be able to move objects that may have seemed heavy on Earth, and effortlessly move from one part of the spacecraft to the other.

Docking with the ISS

After around six hours, the spacecraft can be manoeuvred to dock with the ISS. The docking ports on the spacecraft will need to line up with the ISS, and 12 pairs of docking clips need to connect with the ISS – it's finally time to make your way aboard!

DIY Space Experiment:

MAKE YOUR OWN ROCKET

Find out how forces affect rockets in this fun experiment!

What you need:

- A plastic milk bottle or similar (empty and cleaned) without the lid
- A4 paper
- Scissors
- A pen
- Colouring pens or pencils
- A small plate to draw around
- Sticky tape

What to do:

1 Draw the rocket parts

Place the small plate on the paper and draw around it – this circle will become your rocket body. Next, draw triangles on two corners of the paper, roughly 5 cm x 5 cm – these will be your rocket fins.

2 Cut out the rocket parts

Cut out the outline of the rocket body and the fins. Draw lines to split your rocket body into four equal quarters. Now cut out a quarter of the rocket body and discard this section.

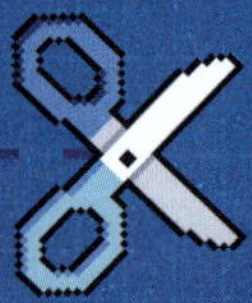

3 Get creative

Decorate the rocket body and fins with pens or pencils.

4 Make a cone

Twist the rocket body into a cone shape and attach with tape.

5 Attach the fins

Attach the rocket fins symmetrically to either side of the main rocket body with tape.

6 Prepare the bottle

Put the rocket on top of the milk bottle. Make sure the bottle is on a flat surface – you are now ready for blast off!

7 Clap your hands

Clap your hands into the milk bottle and watch your rocket fly into the air.

What's the science?

Rockets need a thrust force to overcome Earth's gravity and make it to space. You will have noticed after your rocket launched, it quickly returned to the ground due to the force of gravity. The bigger the thrust force, the further the rocket will travel. You can experiment with this by using different amounts of force (clapping your hands on the bottle gently or more firmly) to see how high your rocket will go.

Mission Log:
[LIVING IN SPACE]

Good job, you've made it to the ISS - your six-month mission in space begins now! You need to get used to new routines and the weightless environment, as this will be your home for a while.

It's time to learn about...

> What's on the ISS
> Your body in space
> Your daily routine
> Keeping fit
> Toilet training
> Keeping clean
> How to spend your free time
> Sleeping
> Waste and recycling
> Liquids in space
> What's on the menu

WHAT'S ON THE ISS?

Apart from Earth, space stations like the ISS are the only other places humans have lived. The ISS is a huge science laboratory orbiting around our planet. Since November 2000, it has been continuously occupied with astronauts from more than 25 different countries. The space for living and working on the ISS is designed for a crew of seven. It is larger than a six-bedroom house, with seven sleeping quarters, two bathrooms, a gym, and a 360-degree view window called the Cupola, which looks towards Earth.

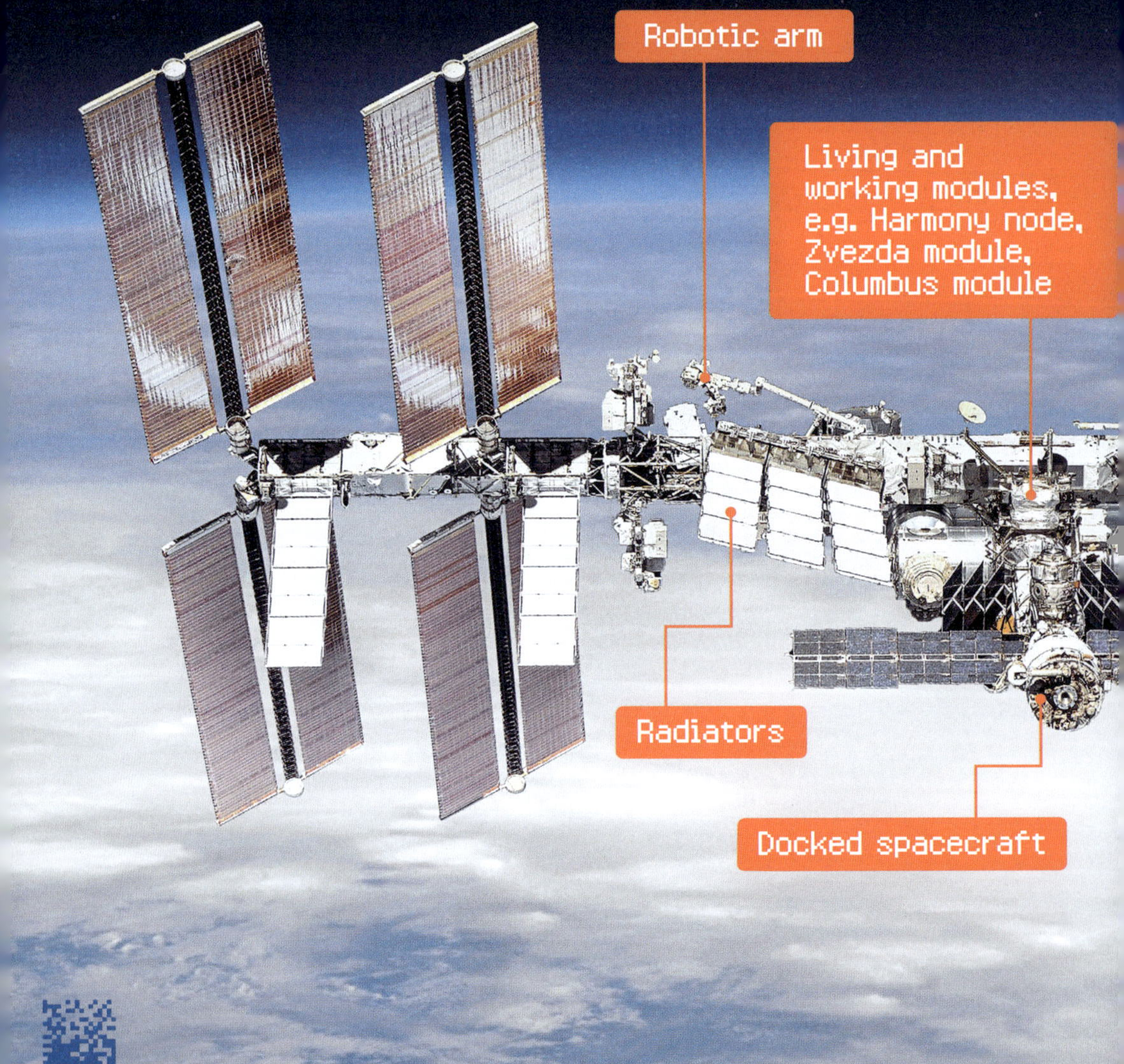

Cupola

The Cupola is one of the most famous sites on the ISS. It's a specially designed observing window for viewing Earth, offering incredible views.

YOUR BODY IN SPACE

Now that you've arrived at the ISS, you'll find that the microgravity environment has a variety of weird and wonderful effects on your body. Some of these will last a few days while you get used to your new home, and others can last for your entire trip to space! Are you ready to put your training to the test?

Feeling queasy

You might feel a little ill in space, a bit like travel sickness. This is called space adaptation syndrome. Scientists think this happens because the fluid in our ears that helps us to balance starts to float around, confusing the brain and making us feel unwell. Most astronauts can adapt within just a few days, but for some this never passes. One famous example was astronaut Jake Garn, who felt really sick throughout his whole trip in space. Now, astronauts use the Garn scale to show how ill they feel: 0 being the least sick and 1 being the most – yuk!

Bones and muscles

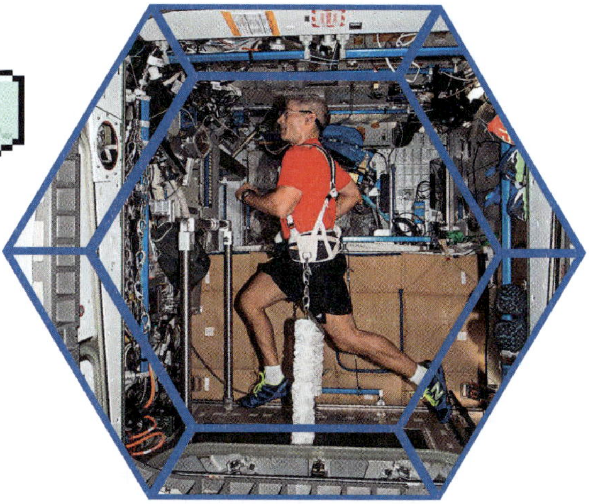

On Earth, your bones and muscles support you against the strong pull of our planet's gravity. But on the ISS, the weightlessness you experience means your bones and muscles don't have to work as hard. That means they get thinner and weaker, which can lead to bone fractures – yikes! In fact, your bones can become 1% less dense for every month you spend in space.

Growing taller

Have you ever wanted to be a bit taller? On Earth, the bones in your spine are squashed together, because of gravity. In space, your spine can relax and expand. This means that on your trip you might find you have grown a whole 5 centimetres taller! This effect isn't permanent and once back on Earth, gravity will return you to your normal height.

Can you work out what your height would be in space?

Chicken legs and puffy face

Whilst on Earth, the blood in our body is pulled downwards and the heart works super hard to move it around our whole body. However, in space, blood shifts to the upper body, giving you the strange look of a puffy and slightly red face, like hanging upside down on the monkey bars. It also makes the legs look thinner, a bit like a chicken, as blood is pushed up through the body.

YOUR DAILY ROUTINE

The ISS works on GMT (Greenwich Mean Time), which is the same time as the UK in the winter and one hour behind the UK in the summer. Because the ISS orbits the Earth every 90 minutes, you see a sunset and sunrise 16 times every 24 hours, so it can be hard to work out how long a day is! Keeping to GMT makes your day more structured. Your day might look something like this...

6-6:30 a.m. > Time to wake up

You will probably wake up somewhere between 6 a.m. and 6:30 a.m. to get ready for your day.

6:30-7 a.m. > Time to get dressed

On the ISS, you can wear the same sorts of clothes as you would on Earth – normally T-shirts and trousers. However, because there is nowhere to do washing, you need to wear clothes for as long as possible. This means that T-shirts get changed once a week, socks every four days, underwear every two days and trousers once a month!

The working day

During the day, you need to complete any experiments you have been assigned. You also have daily and weekly health checks, including eye health and blood tests.

Meals

You have three main meals a day, the same as you would at home. The only difference is the food – it is normally dehydrated and cold, and needs to be heated and rehydrated before you eat it. All the food is pre-made to support your individual needs.

3-5 p.m. > Exercise

To keep fit and healthy in space, you need to exercise between two and two and a half hours a day, using adapted resistance equipment. This will help your muscles and bones stay healthy in a weightless environment. About half of your time is spent on cardio fitness and the other half on weightlifting.

7-10 p.m. > The end of the day

After all of your tasks are finished and you've eaten dinner, you get some free time to read, contact home, listen to music or watch a film, before getting ready for eight hours of sleep.

Always on call

As an astronaut, you are on call 24 hours a day and usually work five and a half days a week.

KEEPING FIT

On the ISS, going to the gym helps keep your muscles and bones strong, and your heart healthy. Certain tasks, like going on a spacewalk for several hours, require strength and good fitness, so exercise is also important for mission readiness. It is also helpful to make sure that you have enough strength and mobility for when you return to Earth and have to work against the force of gravity again. To make sure your body stays in tip-top condition, every day is scheduled with a minimum of two hours of exercise – that's 8% of your time in space!

Advanced Resistive Exercise Device (ARED)

Because free weights would float around on the ISS, the ARED uses vacuum cylinders to create resistance. This simulates weighted exercises like squats, deadlifts and bench presses. The vacuum cylinders are like reverse bicycle pumps. Imagine trying to suck all the air out of a tyre – when there's not much air left (a vacuum), it becomes difficult to pump any more out, so you feel some resistance. This tests your strength.

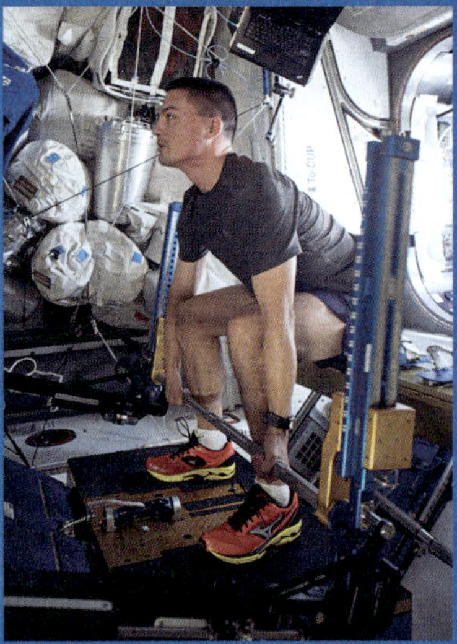

T2 Colbert treadmill

When you run on Earth, you push off the ground with every step. In space, this would result in you floating away! A specially designed treadmill with bungee cords allows you to strap yourself in, and holds you down while you're running. The treadmill also has a system to prevent vibrations from shaking the rest of the ISS.

Stationary bike (CEVIS)

Unlike an exercise bike on Earth, you don't need a seat or handlebars to support your body weight. Instead, you stand upright with your feet strapped into the pedals, using special cycling shoes to stop you from drifting away!

Guinness World Record

In 2016, Tim Peake ran the London Marathon in space on the ISS treadmill. It's the fastest marathon completed in space – his time of 3 hours, 35 minutes and 21 seconds set a Guinness World Record.

Space triathlon

In 2012, Sunita Williams completed the first triathlon in space. She used the T2 treadmill for the running, the CEVIS bike for the cycling, and the ARED weightlifting machine to simulate the swimming section.

TOILET TRAINING

Ever wondered how you go to the toilet in space? The toilet on the ISS was upgraded in 2021 to a new model, costing over £16 million! It was designed to be smaller, lighter and easier to use. All space toilets use suction to stop human waste floating around the spacecraft. Ugh!

Lights, camera, action

Before you travelled to the ISS, you will have practised using the space toilet on Earth. Training toilets have a camera inside, to check you can line yourself up with the seat! A camera isn't needed on the toilet on the ISS – by now, you should be an expert at using the bathroom in space!

Toilets suck!

To make sure you don't end up with poo and wee where you don't want it, you need to use suction to pull it to the right place. The space toilet has two main sections: a hose for wees and a seat for poos. Every astronaut is supplied with their own adaptor that fits into the hose and on the body to give a close fit and avoid any leaks! Using airflow, the toilet pulls the waste away from your body – through the hose for urine or into a plastic bag for poo.

Cleaning up

After you have finished on the toilet, you need to clean up using wet wipes, toilet paper and gloves. You put these in watertight bags. If you have done a poo, you should replace the bag for the next user.

Shooting stars

Once you have filled a poo bag, you drop it into the container (canister) underneath the toilet. Once the canister is full, normally after 30 poos, two things happen. A few might be returned to Earth for testing to make sure you and your crew are healthy. Otherwise, the canisters are shot back to Earth and burnt up in the atmosphere. They won't reach the Earth's surface, but if you look up and see a shooting star, just be wary what you might be wishing on!

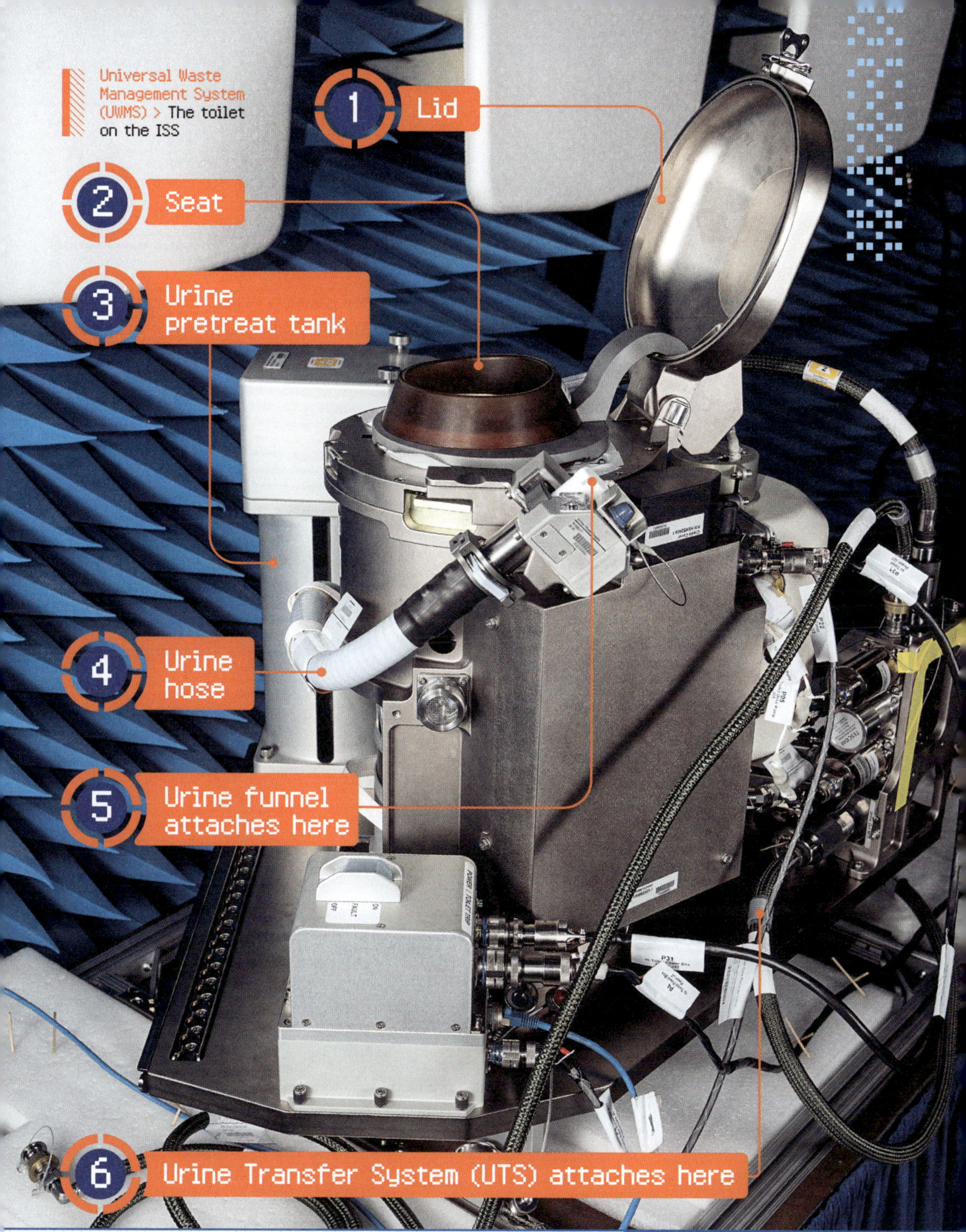

Space isn't glamorous

This may all sound messy and not very glamorous, but using the toilet in space has improved a lot in recent years. In the 1970s, astronauts on the Skylab space station used simple equipment – more similar to a hole in the wall. The crew had to dry their poo before bringing it back to Earth. During the Apollo missions, astronauts used sticky bags they could attach to their bottoms to poo into.

KEEPING CLEAN

There's no running water on the ISS, and opening a window to get some fresh air isn't an option! Without an endless supply of resources, some of the daily activities you perform on Earth need to be adapted in space to keep things clean and safe.

Washing clothes

Water is a precious resource on the ISS and there's no washing machine on board! So you need to wear the same clothes for a few days before throwing them away and getting new ones. Before the mission, you will have worked out what clothes you need to bring, to make sure there's enough to last you during your time on the ISS.

Sweat

Clothes can get quite sweaty because of all the exercise you're doing on the ISS. Some items, like socks and exercise gear, are made with anti-bacterial materials or contain silver/copper fibres. This prevents bacteria which causes odours from growing. The sweat on clothes is left to evaporate – the water vapour is collected through the air conditioning and water recovery system, and recycled into drinking water!

Haircuts and brushing teeth

You can use razors and hair clippers to keep you looking your best. They come with a suction device to catch any stray hairs and prevent them from floating around the ISS. You can also brush your teeth as normal, but you need to spit the toothpaste into a hand cloth or swallow the edible toothpaste to help reduce waste.

Showering

On past space stations like NASA's Skylab, there was a shower with a spray nozzle for water. However, it took more than two hours to have a shower because stray water droplets had to be vacuumed up to prevent damage to equipment. On the ISS, you use wet wipes or take 'sponge baths' using towels, water pouches with dispensers and no-rinse soap. You also use no-rinse shampoo – the airflow systems on the ISS help to collect any excess moisture in the environment.

Dead skin

Because you don't use the soles of your feet much in space, when you're floating around, they become smooth and soft – it's like a free pedicure! However, that means the dead, hard skin starts coming off after a few weeks. You have to be careful taking your socks off, otherwise lots of flakes of skin start spreading around the station! In microgravity, they don't fall to the floor; they hang around until they find their way to one of the air filters.

Station hygiene

Just like at home, the ISS needs to be kept clean. In addition to daily tidying, every Saturday you might spend two to four hours doing housekeeping. You use anti-microbial wipes to clean surfaces, especially the toilet area, and vacuum the air vents and filters to clean dust and debris collected from the air. You also need to sanitise high-touch areas like handrails, communication equipment and the kitchen area, known as the galley.

FREE TIME

On the ISS, you don't have lots of free time each day, but there is the chance to spend time doing the things you enjoy in a completely different way. Reading a book while floating, speaking to friends and family and watching films are all things you can enjoy doing on the ISS.

Sightseeing

For many astronauts, looking back at planet Earth from the Cupola observing window is a favourite pastime. These unique views are rarely seen by other humans, so the module is a popular spot for sightseeing and photography.

Personal space

On the ISS you have your own living quarters, where you can keep your personal belongings. As well as a laptop for communication, work and watching films and sport, you can bring special belongings from home, such as photos, books, an instrument or a special toy. In your living quarters, you can have some time to yourself away from the rest of the crew.

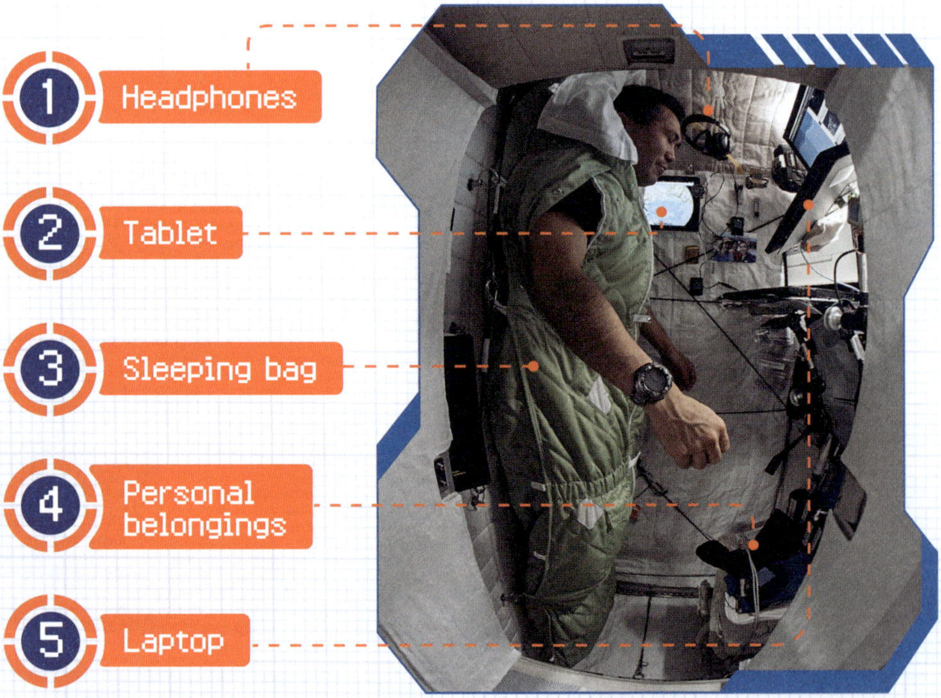

Time to celebrate

The ISS always has people living on it, so you celebrate the important dates you would on Earth. During holidays and special events, you also have time to relax. This is a photo of NASA astronauts Nick Hague and Suni Williams sharing some festive snacks on Christmas Eve on board the ISS.

Playing tricks

On board the ISS, you might play tricks on other members of the crew to pass the time. This photo shows astronaut Scott Kelly dressed as a gorilla for his birthday, chasing his crewmate Tim Peake around the space station.

Sports in space

If you're a sports fan, you can watch your favourite team play a match, or have a game of football around the station. In microgravity, a game like football has a whole new level of difficulty!

SLEEPING

With a busy schedule of activities to perform throughout the day, you'll have roughly eight hours of time scheduled for sleep, to give your mind and body time to rest.

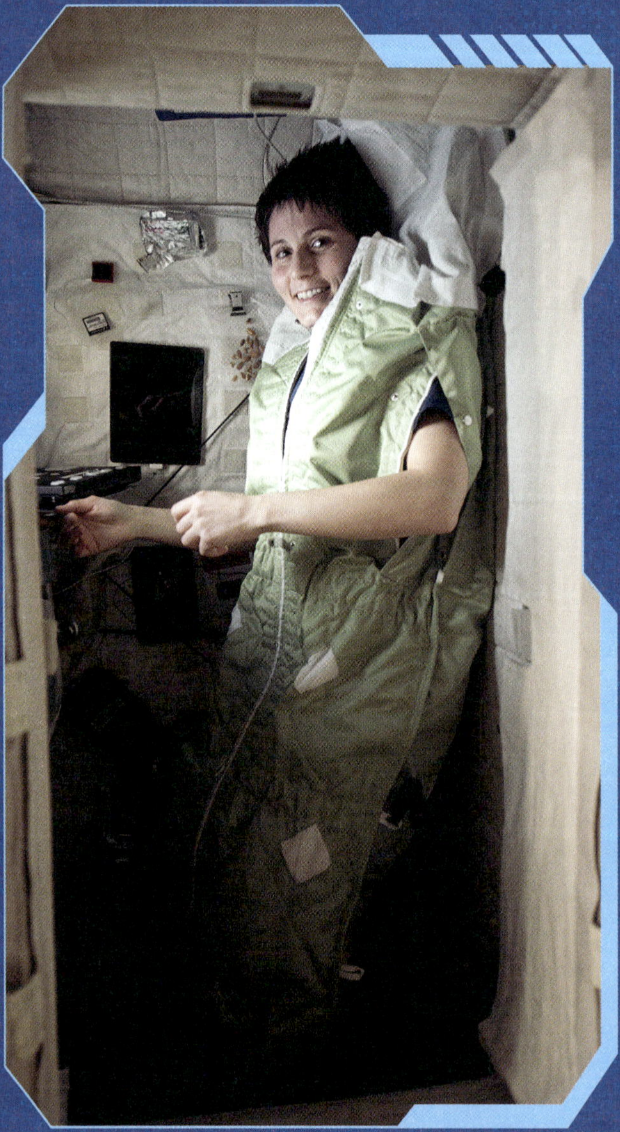

Where do you sleep?

There are seven permanent sleeping areas on the ISS, each about the size of a phone box – four in the American segment (Harmony node), two in the Russian segment (Zvezda module) and one in the European segment (Columbus module). If there are more than seven astronauts on board, sleeping arrangements are improvised. For example, you might have to sleep inside the docked spacecraft, or attach a sleeping bag to an unused wall, the floor, or a ceiling in the station! The most people that have been aboard the ISS at any one time is 13 – sleeping arrangements got pretty inventive!

How do you sleep?

Each private sleeping area has a specially designed sleeping bag, and there is a little space to put your personal items from home. To stop you floating off as you sleep, the bags are fastened to the wall – vertically! While there's no real sense of up or down in space, you technically sleep standing up.

As you don't need to rest on a surface, no pillows or mattresses are needed to be comfortable. However, some astronauts use a pillow so that they feel at home.

The sleeping bags are more like soft, wearable cocoons than the traditional sealed bags used here on Earth. They have holes for the arms, so you might find that your arms float up, and you look like a zombie while you sleep!

Best night's sleep ever?

Sleeping on the ISS can be a challenge. There are ventilation fans and other noisy equipment, artificial light from inside the ISS and sunlight beaming in every 90 minutes. However, you can use earplugs and eye masks to help, and the ISS uses dimmed lighting during sleeping hours. In fact, in space you might have the best night's sleep you've ever had! Without the pressure and weight of your body pressing into a mattress, there's no need to constantly change positions to stay comfortable.

WASTE AND RECYCLING

The ISS is an expensive place to send rockets and so it is important that as much as possible is recycled on board, to make it as efficient as possible. One of the ways this is done is to recycle more than 80% of water used on the ISS – this includes urine, sweat and breath. Yuck!

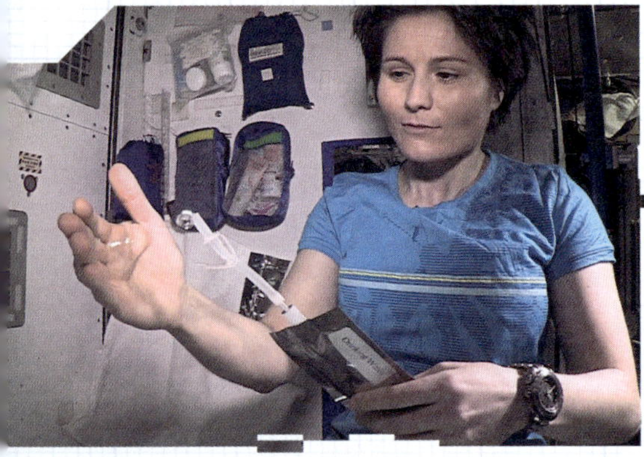

Recycling wee

Since 2009, the space station has recycled astronauts' wee to make sure very few resources are wasted. To do this, the waste water is passed through filtration systems to take out impurities. Through innovation and improvements, the space station can now recycle nearly 98% of urine. This isn't as horrible as it sounds – the water is really clean; better than some of the drinking water on Earth!

Re-using breath and sweat

Both breath and sweat are collected by the environmental systems on the space station. Like giant dehumidifiers, they take in moisture from the air and then cool it into water droplets. It can then be filtered in the same way as urine, to make clean and safe drinking water for you and your crew!

Refabricator > 3D printer used for recycling plastic waste into new tools

Plastic recycling

To reduce waste on the ISS, plastic and old parts are recycled to make them usable for 3D printing. A machine known as the Refabricator can recycle plastic waste and use it to create new tools and equipment.

Taking out the rubbish

The ISS creates 2,500 kg of rubbish each year. This includes food packaging, clothing and wet wipes. Recycling as much of this as possible reduces waste and makes the space station more efficient.
If any waste can't be recycled, it is jettisoned (thrown or dropped) from the ISS towards Earth. As it makes its way through the Earth's atmosphere, it burns up before it reaches the surface.

LIQUIDS IN SPACE

On Earth, due to gravity, liquids take up the shape of their container, whether this is a glass, a bowl, or even a canal or river. In microgravity, liquid molecules cling to each other to form a sphere. If water wasn't contained in pouches or drums, it would float around the ISS in football-shaped blobs! So how do you deal with liquids in space?

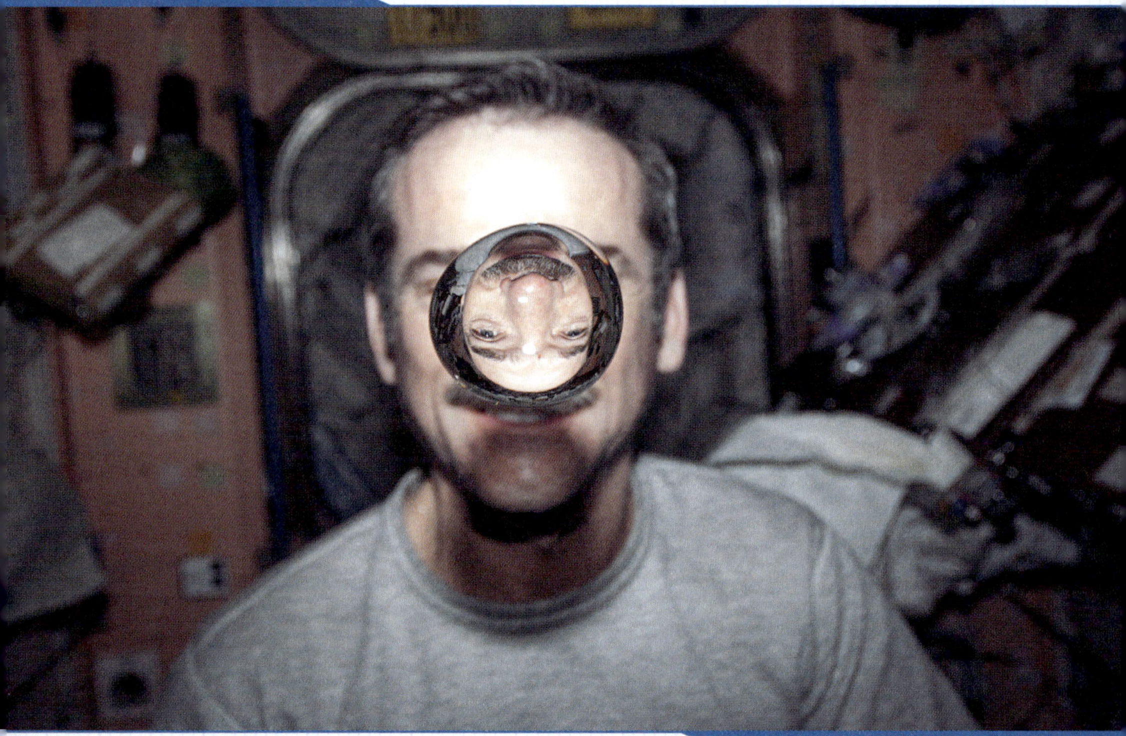

Sticky water

Without gravity to pull water away from an object in space, it will stick to different surfaces like skin, clothing or equipment. This means that you can't cry properly in space. If you do, your eyes will water, but the tears will stay stuck to your eyeballs!

Wring it out

Imagine you have a cloth full of water and you want to wring out the excess water before you wipe your face. You can wring the cloth as hard as you like, but the water will be stuck to the cloth's surface – and probably your hand too!

Freezing wee

Before water was recycled on the ISS, all liquid waste, including wee, was removed from the space station to get rid of it. Once the water went outside, it would instantly freeze into tiny particles. Some astronauts reported that it looked like sparklers in space!

Drinking in microgravity

In space, you drink water out of special containers. This makes sure that no water is floating around to get into equipment or electronics. The containers are specially designed plastic pouches. They can be re-filled, and they have special straws fitted with lids to avoid water escaping. Here are some astronauts enjoying their first recycled water on the ISS.

Mixing liquids and oil

On Earth, if you mix liquids and oil together and leave them for long enough, you will see them start to separate. The less dense oil will float to the surface. Why not try this at home and see if it works with water and vegetable oil? In space, however, because of the lack of gravity, the oil will stay suspended in droplets within the water.

WHAT'S ON THE MENU?

To make sure you stay fit and healthy in space, your meals are carefully selected and packaged to ensure you have a nutritious and varied diet. However, you can choose some of your menu from a range of American, European, Russian and Japanese food options.

Food on the ISS

Without a supermarket within driving distance, and no fridge on the ISS, fresh food is a treat. A limited supply of fruit and vegetables arrives with each visiting vehicle, but must be eaten within a few days. Then it's back to the usual pouches or packet foods prepared for eating in space. These items are made in a very clean environment to avoid contamination and have a long expiry date.

Most food on board is:

Rehydratable (you add hot or cold water before eating or drinking)
> for example, noodles, rice, drinks like green tea

Thermostabilised (pouched or canned foods that can be heated in the food warmer before eating)
> for example, ravioli, curry, puddings

Natural and semi-dried (foods that can be eaten as is)
> for example, tortillas, dried fruit, beef jerky

Add some sauce

Because microgravity causes fluids to shift to your upper body, you may often feel congested. This can reduce your sense of taste and smell, similar to when you have a cold. As a result, food tastes blander, so spices and bold flavours are used to make meals more appetising. You can also use condiments like soy sauce, ketchup, liquid salt and pepper.

Great British Space Dinner

For his 2015–2016 mission to the ISS, British astronaut Tim Peake had some space comfort foods specially designed by chef Heston Blumenthal. The 'Great British Space Dinner' menu included a tinned bacon sandwich, sausage and mash with gravy, a Sunday roast designed as a pie and even Eton mess – a classic British dessert.

Pizza delivery!

In 2001, the Russian Space Agency teamed up with Pizza Hut to have a salami-topped pizza delivered to the ISS. It had to be modified to meet the space food safety requirements and cost $1 million!

Food from around the world

Creating and sharing food together on the ISS boosts morale and gives a family feeling away from home. Using everyday items on the ISS like rice, spam, fish, seaweed, crackers and different condiments, astronauts have created space sushi. Other flavourful Japanese menu items like chicken ramen, rice crackers and mackerel with miso sauce are popular among many astronauts.

DIY Space Experiment:

STOMACH OF AN ASTRONAUT

Find out what happens to an astronaut's stomach in microgravity – and why you might not want to burp in space!

What you need:

- A two-litre plastic bottle (empty and cleaned) with the lid
- Water
- Orange juice or orange squash
- Two handfuls of raisins or sultanas

What to do:

1 Add water

Half fill the plastic bottle with water – this will be the liquid inside the astronaut's stomach.

2 Add orange juice

Now add the orange juice or squash – this will be the stomach acid inside the astronaut's stomach.

3 Add the raisins

Add the raisins, making sure there are enough so that you can see them at the bottom of the bottle – this will be the food inside the astronaut's stomach.

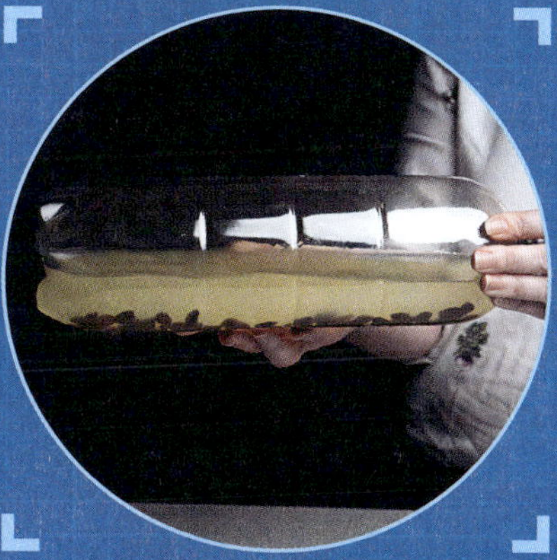

4 Let it settle

Screw the lid tightly onto the bottle. You should see that the food, liquid and air all layer up in that order inside the stomach. This is how your stomach would be on Earth.

5 Shake it up

Now, holding the bottle horizontally, give it a really big shake. You should see that the liquid, the food and the air (bubbles) all mix up together. This is what would happen to the astronaut's stomach in space!

What's the science?

On Earth, because of gravity, solids sink to the bottom of your stomach, while gases rise to the top and liquids settle in the middle. Density describes how heavy something is for its size. And because solids are usually denser (heavier for their size) than liquids, which in turn are denser than gases, the denser solids sink downwards and the gases sit at the top.

But in the microgravity of space, objects float around – they don't sink or rise due to their density. That means everything is mixed up in your stomach, and if you burp, it's not just gas that comes up – it's the liquid and solid parts too!

Mission Log:
[WORKING IN SPACE]

Now that you're familiar with your daily routine and life on the ISS, it's time to start your mission-specific research and activities.

Carry on reading to find out about...

> Spacewalk suits
> What to expect on a spacewalk
> Animals in space
> Experiments in microgravity
> Space debris
> Medical research in space

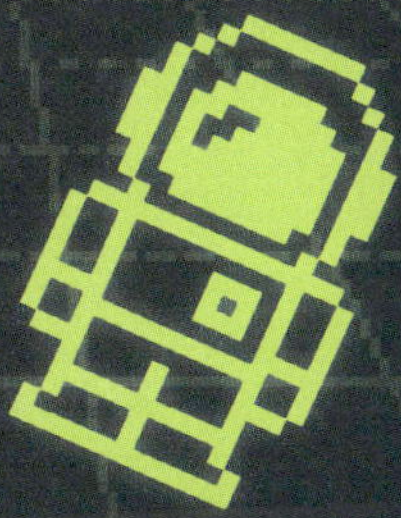

Spacewalks:

WHAT TO WEAR

A spacewalk or Extravehicular Activity (EVA) is the opportunity to walk outside the ISS or spacecraft. The environment outside the spacecraft is very different to inside, so you need to wear a special spacesuit to protect you. The Extravehicular Mobility Unit (EMU) is the NASA spacesuit used on the ISS to conduct spacewalks.

1 Maximum absorbency layer

The maximum absorbency layer is the first thing you need to put on before a spacewalk. It is similar to an adult-sized nappy and can absorb one hundred times its own weight in water. It's useful in case you need a wee during a spacewalk – the last thing you want is wee floating inside your spacesuit!

2 Cooling/ventilation layer

Putting on a cooling and ventilation layer is the next step in getting dressed for a spacewalk. This has water pipes that cross over the body, carrying cool water to keep your body at a constant temperature. You can tweak this with the dials and controls on the front of your suit.

3 Life support

The Portable Life Support System (PLSS) backpack provides essential supplies like oxygen for up to eight hours.

4 Patches

On the front and the shoulders of the suit, you can display mission patches and your country's flag patch.

5 Kevlar

The suit is made of Kevlar, a hardwearing fabric used in bullet-proof vests. This avoids tears or holes in the suit.

6 Helmet

The helmet includes lights for working in dark conditions, a camera to record your work, and a reflective visor to protect you from the Sun.

Extravehicular Mobility Unit >
ESA astronaut Alexander Gerst
in his EMU

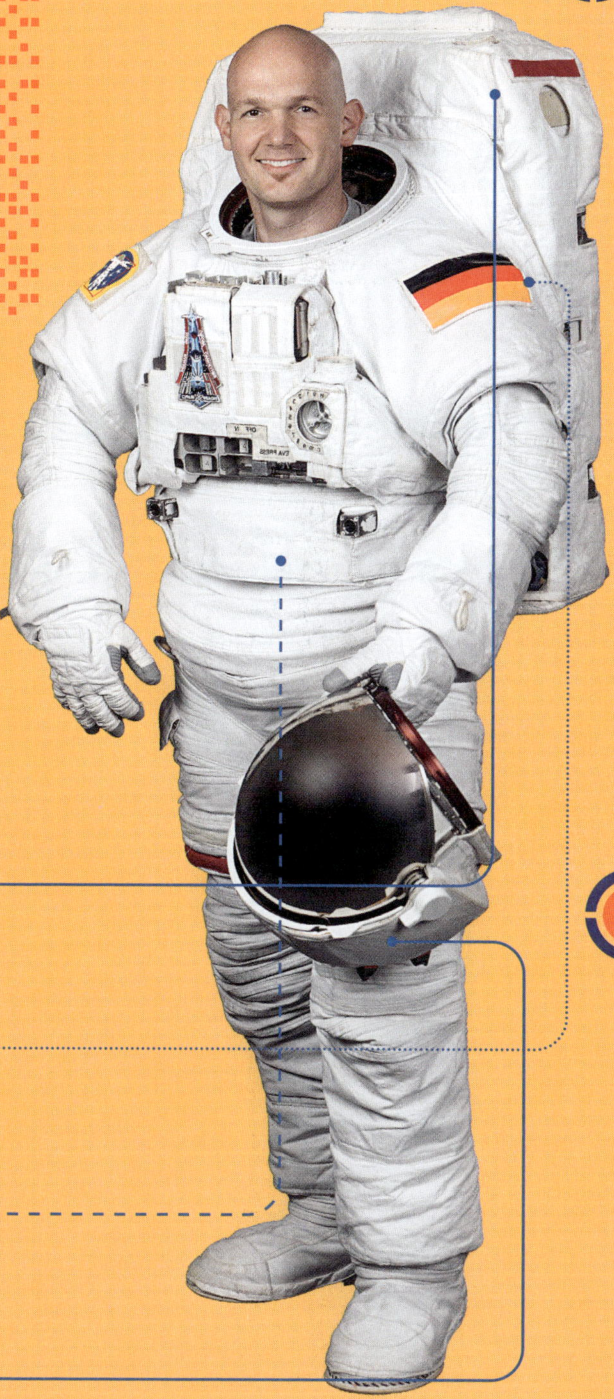

7 Snoopy cap

You'll wear a specialised helmet liner under your helmet, which contains microphones and built-in earphones for communicating with other crew members and Mission Control. It's often nicknamed the 'Snoopy cap' because its white and black design looks a bit like the ears and head of the cartoon character Snoopy.

8 Layers

There can be as many as 14–16 layers that make up an EVA spacesuit, which also includes a bladder layer to help maintain the correct air pressure within the suit.

WHAT TO EXPECT ON A SPACEWALK

You might need to go on a spacewalk to complete some technical repair work on the ISS, or conduct research or experiments. This kind of walk isn't relaxing – as well as wearing a special spacesuit, you need to make sure that you don't venture too far and that you look out for micrometeoroids!

Repairs

The outside of the space station is constantly bombarded with micrometeoroids or space debris. Most of the debris is around 3 mm in size, but if it is larger than 1 cm, it can cause serious damage to the outside of the station. One way to avoid collisions is to manoeuvre the ISS out of the way – larger objects over 5 cm can be detected and tracked from Earth. If there is impact from smaller particles, you may need to repair the outside of the ISS. You may also need to do general repairs or upgrades from time to time. For example, on Christmas Eve in 2013, astronauts completed a spacewalk to repair a faulty pump.

Invented for space

Whether it's a headset for communication or a power tool needed during a spacewalk – cordless, portable, battery-operated technologies were things that NASA developed for use in space exploration. Every day, we now all make use of many cordless devices, like drills and vacuum cleaners.

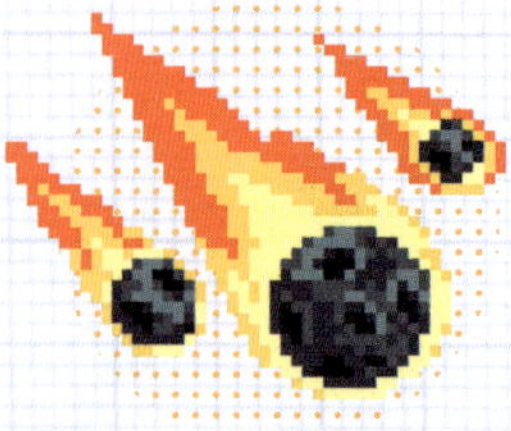

Look out!

Even though space debris is tiny, because the space station, and you, are orbiting at more than 28,000 kilometres per hour, it can have enough energy to pierce a hole in your suit when you are on a spacewalk. This can cause the air to leak from your suit and reduce the pressure inside. So it is important that the outer layer of your suit is made from a very strong material, like Kevlar.

The vacuum of space

Outside the space station there is no air, so your spacesuit needs to provide you with everything you need to breathe and stay alive. In space, liquids boil at a much lower temperature; the reduced air pressure means that water needs less energy to change to gas. This is not good news when you are doing a spacewalk, as nearly 70 per cent of your body is made of water! So the bladder layers are very important in a spacesuit, stopping air from escaping from the suit.

Tethering

When completing a spacewalk, it is important not to get too far away from the main spacecraft. You use tethers to keep you attached – these are like large ropes attached to both you and the spacecraft. They stop you from floating away and becoming lost in space. You can also use the small jets on your suit's backpack system to help manoeuvre you if you move too far from the main spacecraft. In 1965, Ed White was the first American to go for a walk in space. Look how he is tethered, using the gold-tape-covered cord.

What research would you like to carry out on a spacewalk?

Experiments

Spacewalks can be a way of conducting research about space. On previous missions, astronauts have conducted tests to find out if micro-organisms exiting the space station through vents can survive in space. They have also looked at how much radiation the human body receives while completing a spacewalk. These types of experiments help to make space safer for the future.

ANIMALS IN SPACE

Some animals might travel with you to the ISS. Many different animals have been to the space station before to see how microgravity affects them, how they adapt to space, and whether they could live in space for a long time. Scientists also look at the changes in these animals' behaviours while they're in space. This can help them learn how humans might be able to adapt for future long-term missions to Mars and beyond.

Golden orb spiders

In 2011, two golden orb spiders called Gladys and Esmerelda were launched to the ISS on the Endeavour Space Shuttle. On Earth, these spiders normally weave non-symmetrical webs so they have a spot for watching their prey. In microgravity, they created more symmetrical webs when they were in the dark, but webs similar to the ones on Earth when the lights were on. This helped scientists understand that in the absence of gravity, they use light to help them in their work.

Bobtail squid

In 2021, 128 glow-in-the-dark, baby bobtail squid were sent to space to see how they would react to microgravity conditions. A squid's immune system is similar to that of humans; it relies on microbes for good health. So this was an important experiment to help understand how microbes in humans might be affected by long-term space missions. Scientists studied the squid to see how microgravity affected their interactions with their microbes. They found that microbes were needed to make sure the squid were happy and healthy.

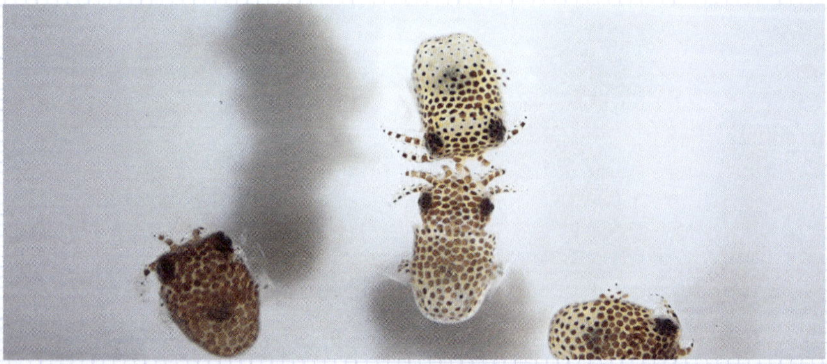

Water bears

Tardigrades, or water bears, have been sent to the ISS on a few different occasions since 2007 to study how they survive the harsh conditions of space. Here on Earth, tardigrades are a type of microscopic organism known as an extremophile, because they live and thrive in extreme conditions. In 2011, tardigrades were sent to the ISS as part of an experiment called TARDIKISS (Tardigrades in Space). The experiment concluded that they were not significantly affected by the radiation or microgravity experienced in space, and they survived.

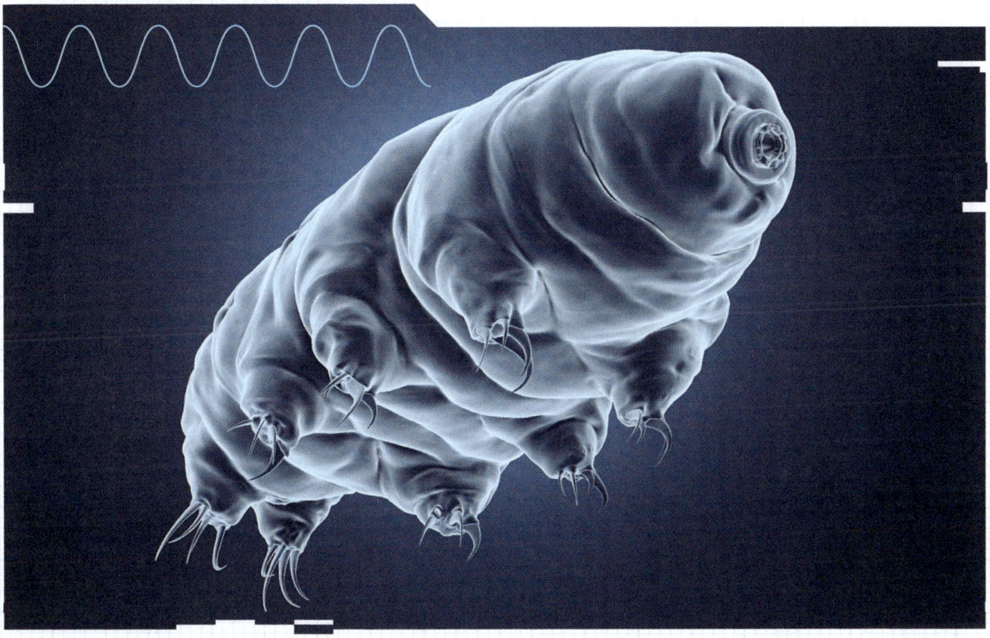

Fish in space

The Japan Aerospace Exploration Agency (JAXA) put zebrafish and medaka fish in a specially designed fish tank on the ISS to see how they adapted to microgravity. Just like humans, their bone density decreased in just 10 days. They also started to swim in unusual patterns, not seeming to know where was up and down, and circling around. However, in a similar way to humans, they adapted after a few days in space.

EXPERIMENTS IN MICROGRAVITY

Microgravity provides a unique environment to carry out science experiments. On Earth, gravity creates unwanted effects when you're testing things. But in space, physical, chemical and biological processes can be studied without unwanted interference. You could be involved in cutting-edge research while working on the ISS – what are you most excited about and interested in investigating?

Fire in space

FLEX (Flame Extinguishment Experiment) was a NASA experiment designed to understand how flames spread and are extinguished in space, and how microgravity affects combustion – the reaction which is used to power rockets. Studies showed that flames burn slower in space and are spherical, not teardrop-shaped, because hot gases do not rise in microgravity. FLEX also discovered 'cool flames', where fuel droplets burn at low temperatures with an invisible flame, even after the initial, hot fire is extinguished. This research is helping with fire safety and engine efficiency on Earth.

Flame experiment > a candle burning in normal gravity (left) and microgravity (right)

Growing specialised cells

Stem cells are cells which haven't yet picked a job – they can become any other type of cell. They are needed by your body for repair, growth and staying healthy. The Italian Space Agency (ASI) looked at how stem cells could be used to create osteoblasts – the cells responsible for bone formation. Scientists could use this research to help fight the bone density loss that astronauts experience in space, and also use it to treat osteoporosis (a bone-weakening disease) on Earth.

Space garden

The Vegetable Production System, known as Veggie, is a space garden on the ISS. Its main aim is to help NASA study plant growth in microgravity. However, Veggie also means that you and your crew can have a small amount of fresh food in your diet. And like gardening on Earth, it can help the crew's well-being on the ISS. Veggie uses a soil-free method of growing plants, which draws water and nutrients directly to the roots. As there is no sunlight, it uses LED lighting to trigger photosynthesis, which is how plants make their food. Lettuce, cabbage and kale have been grown in the space garden. Although most plants are not grown to be eaten, astronauts have tried space-grown foods like lettuce and chilli peppers.

SPACE DEBRIS

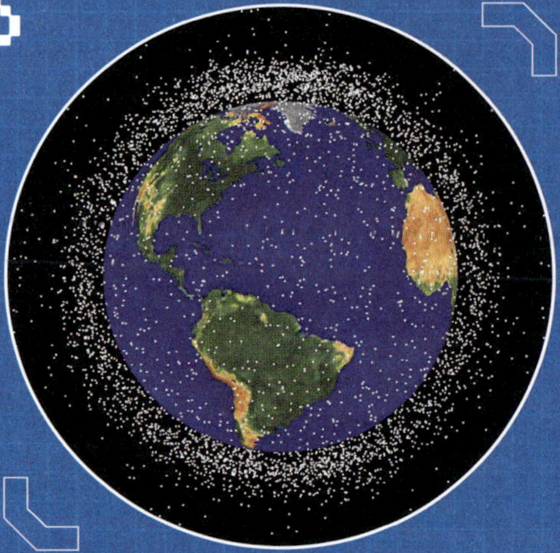

The ISS travels around the planet in low Earth orbit (LEO). Like a busy motorway, this orbit is filled with many other satellites, missions, and millions of pieces of space debris! Space debris includes satellites that are no longer working, used rocket stages, fragments from collisions, tools dropped by astronauts, and even flecks of paint.

Space hazards

There are over 40,000 objects orbiting in LEO that are being tracked, but only about a quarter of these are working satellites or equipment. It's estimated that there are over 50,000 pieces of space debris larger than 10 cm, over 1 million pieces bigger than 1 cm and over 100 million fragments over 1 mm, with countless smaller objects.

Because these pieces of space debris are travelling at around 28,000 kilometres per hour, they are a real hazard – a collision at that speed could cause a hole in the station (like a bullet travelling through thin metal). A major incident like this could threaten your mission on the ISS!

Potential evacuation

In 2024, there was an accidental explosion of a Russian satellite which had stopped working a few years earlier. This caused a few hundred pieces of space debris to be created close to the ISS. It resulted in ISS crew members taking shelter in their docked spacecraft. When the station is at risk of being struck by space debris, astronauts are instructed to prepare for an evacuation by getting into their docked spacecraft (which is like their lifeboat), so they're ready to leave if necessary. Would you remain calm in a situation like this?

The Kessler Syndrome

An idea put forward by NASA scientist Donald Kessler in 1978, known as the Kessler Syndrome, is that as the amount of space debris increases, collisions will become more likely. Each collision will create more debris, leading to a runaway chain reaction – like a line of falling dominoes! This will ultimately make LEO unusable for satellites and future space missions. If the problem of space debris isn't tackled now, this might become a real and major crisis within the next few decades.

Debris removal

To help clear up space debris, or junk, missions are being developed and tested on the ISS that use robotic arms, nets, and even harpoons, to drag it closer to Earth, where it can burn up in the atmosphere. Many UK companies are leading research in this area. Another idea being developed is to attach a magnetic docking plate to every satellite before it launches, so that at the end of its life it can be used to pull the satellite out of orbit.

MEDICAL RESEARCH

Astronauts carry out experiments on the ISS to develop scientific knowledge – but did you know that as an astronaut, you also become the experiment? While in space, your health will be monitored and compared to your condition before and after being in space. This helps scientists better understand the impacts of being in space on the human body.

3D printed organs

Using a 3D printer and bio-ink, astronauts have experimented with growing human tissues and organs in space. Critically ill patients on Earth may sometimes need an organ transplant – but what if you could simply print off and replace a person's body parts using 3D-printed tissues made from the injured person's own cells? In microgravity, this could be easier and cheaper.

Vision changes

Two-thirds of astronauts experience changes to their vision during their space mission. Fluid shifting towards the upper body, as a result of microgravity, can cause the eyeball to flatten and the optic nerve to swell. While some symptoms of this condition resolve when you return to Earth, others may be permanent or last for months. New research has begun to try and help reduce these changes, like special goggles and bodysuits.

Case study > Mark and Scott Kelly

Identical twins Mark (left) and Scott Kelly (right) were part of a year-long study from March 2015 to March 2016, to see what impacts space has on the human body. As identical twins with the same genes and DNA, the study provided scientists with an ideal point for comparison – Scott spent a year on the ISS and Mark remained on Earth.

What the study found

1 Immune system

Scott's immune system in space responded to vaccines just as well as Mark's did on Earth.

2 Mental health

Scott's mental health remained stable, showing that being in space doesn't drastically change how you think, feel or behave.

3 Blood volume

Scott's blood volume decreased in space. This is the total amount of blood in the body. An average human adult has five litres of blood.

4 Biological age

Scott's biological age (how old your body acts) increased after coming back from space.

5 Bone density

Scott's bone density decreased in microgravity. This improved after he came back to Earth, but some parts of his body didn't recover to pre-flight levels.

Conclusions

Whilst some of these changes don't seem to have had a huge impact, on longer missions things like biological age, bone density and blood volume could have major effects on your health – so astronauts' health will need to be monitored long after they return from space.

Why your mission is so important

Your mission to the ISS won't be risk-free, but you will be contributing to vital science that will one day make long-term space travel beyond the ISS safe and possible for future astronauts.

DIY Space Experiment:
GROW SPACE FOOD

Imagine biting into a fresh strawberry while floating in the ISS! Growing plants in space can be tricky without natural sunlight, easy access to water, and lots of soil – but scientists have been finding ways to get around these challenges. Have a go at growing your own space food!

What you need:

- A clear plastic bottle (550 ml, empty and cleaned) without the lid
- Scissors
- Small pebbles or marbles (for drainage)
- Potting mix
- Growing medium (like cotton wool)
- Fast-growing seeds (such as cress, rocket or herbs)
- Water
- A sunny spot or a grow light

What to do:

1 Prepare the bottle

Using scissors, carefully cut the bottle in half (you may need an adult to help with this part). Turn the top half of the bottle upside down and place it inside the bottom half of the bottle.

2 Create a drainage layer

Next, add a layer of small pebbles or marbles to the top section of the bottle. This will help with drainage and prevent the roots from sitting in water.

3 Add the potting mix

On top of the drainage layer, add a few centimetres of potting mix.

4 Add the growing medium

Next, fluff up the cotton wool or growing medium and place it on top of the potting mix. This will provide support for the plants.

5 Plant the seeds

Make small holes in the growing medium and plant a few seeds according to the instructions on the seed packet.

6 Cover the seeds

Cover the seeds lightly with another layer of potting mix.

7 Add water

Fill the bottle with water until it reaches just below the first soil layer, ensuring that the roots can absorb the water but that the plant itself is not submerged.

8 Find a sunny spot

Place your bottle in a sunny location or under a grow light. Make sure it gets plenty of light for the plants to grow.

9 Observe and care for your plants

Over the next few weeks, observe your plants as they grow. Check the water level regularly and add more water as needed to keep the roots moist.

Mission Log:
[BACK TO EARTH]

Your mission on the ISS has come to an end. Get ready to begin your journey back to Earth.

At this point, you'll need to be prepared for...

> Saying farewell
> The return to Earth
> Touchdown
> Wearing a hydrosuit
> An emergency rescue
> Readjusting to Earth
> Going home
> Recovery and rehabilitation
> Life after space

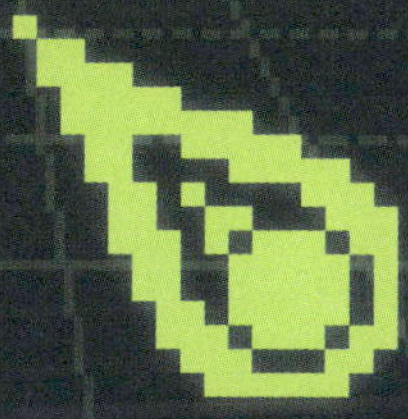

TIME TO GO

Now that your time on the ISS has come to an end, you'll need to get everything ready for your return trip home. So pack up your things and say farewell to your friends!

Packing

Before leaving the ISS, you need to pack your personal belongings and make sure you don't forget anything – you can't pop back! You also need to pack up any scientific equipment used for your experiments. You'll have an inventory, or checklist, to make sure that everything you should have is in the correct place and packaged correctly. The return home can be a bumpy ride – you'll need to make sure everything is well packed so it survives the trip.

Handing over

At the end of your time on the ISS, you need to officially hand over your duties to the crew, or new astronauts arriving on the ISS. A formal change of command ceremony takes place when an outgoing commander hands over responsibility to a new commander before they leave. During the ceremony, they pass over the gold key to the ISS.

Saying goodbye

You have spent six months on the ISS working with colleagues from across the globe – they will have likely become good friends. It is now time to say goodbye, and this can be quite emotional. Goodbyes are often recorded and live streamed with Mission Control. It's your last chance to grab a hug, a handshake or a selfie before you leave for home!

RETURN TO EARTH

Next, it's time to get back into your spacesuit. You should once again be wearing a pressure suit, like the IVA suit you wore for lift-off. This will protect you from emergencies relating to lack of pressure on the return trip. Strap in and get ready for the ride home!

Undocking

First, the spacecraft needs to be undocked from the rest of the space station. To do this, your crew need to close the main hatch from the inside. Then, once everyone is aboard, astronauts in the ISS will close the hatch from their side. Your crew will go through final checks, including pressure testing. The command is given to undock and large metal clips that keep the spacecraft in place are released – this takes up to 3 minutes. Gentle 'pushers' push the spacecraft away – you are now slowly drifting away from the ISS. You will be home in about four hours!

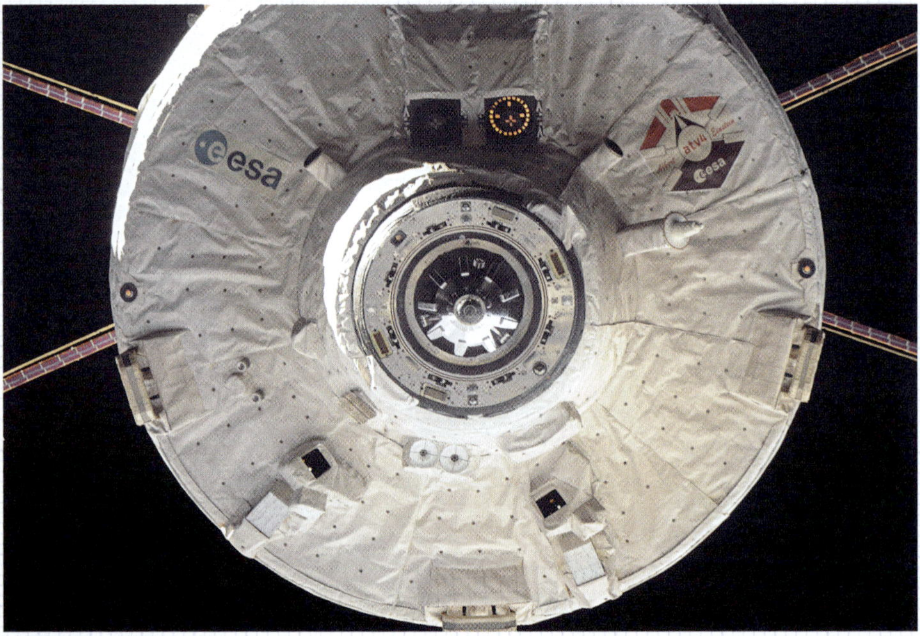

Turn on the jets!

Once you are 20 metres from the ISS, it is time to turn on small jets on the side of the spacecraft. This increases your speed and gets the spacecraft into a position that is a safe distance from the ISS. At this point, the spacecraft is still at a similar altitude to the space station.

The de-orbit burn

Soon, the spacecraft is far enough away from the ISS to initiate a procedure called the de-orbit burn. This burn will decrease the speed of the spacecraft and allow it to enter Earth's atmosphere, which will slow it down further.

Heat shields

On the return to Earth, the spacecraft needs to move through the layers of gases in the Earth's atmosphere. These gases cause pressure and heat on the outside of the spacecraft, which reaches approximately 2,000°C – this is about ten times as hot as your oven at home! To protect you inside, the outside of the spacecraft is covered in specially insulated heat shielding material. The material itself will heat up and partly burn, but it removes the heat away from the main body of the spacecraft. The heat shielding is often black to help radiate some of the heat away from the spacecraft.

Invented for space

Aerogel was initially designed for insulating space vehicles and preventing them from getting too hot. This lightweight material has now found a use in tennis racquets and cosmetic products like moisturising creams.

Vibrations

During the launch to the ISS, you would have felt vibrations and G-force pushing on your body. Making your way back to Earth will also make you feel these things! On re-entry into the Earth's atmosphere, the craft is travelling at 28,000 kilometres per hour – as the speed reduces (like emergency braking in a car), you'll experience this high G-force again, similar to during launch.

TOUCHDOWN

The last part of the journey to Earth is the landing or touchdown. The spacecraft has been travelling extremely fast, but now needs to be slowed down ready to land.

Parachutes

One way this can be done is with parachutes. These deploy and open up to increase air resistance, slowing the descent of the spacecraft. At the last moment before touchdown, small thrusters, known as retrorockets, fire to reduce the speed to a more manageable 5 kilometres per hour. Even so, there will still be a bumpy end to your landing!

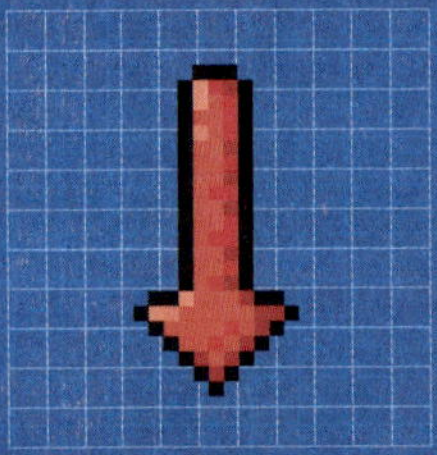

Vertical landing

Rockets such as the SpaceX Falcon 9 and Blue Origin's New Glenn land vertically, using retrorockets firing down to reduce the speed of the landing spacecraft. This uses more fuel than parachutes and creates a controlled stop to the landing.

Runway landing

The NASA Space Shuttle was one of the only crewed spacecraft to land on a runway, rather than on water or vertically. It landed in a similar way to an aeroplane. After it touched down it, it was slowed using a parachute.

Sea landing

Also known as splashdown, some spacecraft land in a big body of water, like the ocean. Parachutes slow the spacecraft down so that it can safely land. The water cushions and supports the spacecraft – you will float until the recovery team collects you!

Recovery

Recovery teams are multi-skilled, highly trained people, ready to collect and potentially rescue you from wherever you land! They are positioned near to the expected landing site of the spacecraft, and ready to move to an alternative site should the spacecraft land in a slightly different place. If the spacecraft lands on water, a recovery ship gets close to the site, ready to hoist it on deck. Should the spacecraft land outside of the country it's from, the team are ready to coordinate with different nations.

Time for a check-up

On land, recovery trucks race to the landing site. Members of the team are medically trained to be able to support you on your arrival back to Earth. When you first arrive, your body will not be used to Earth's gravity, and your bones and muscles will be weak. Once you have been checked over by a doctor, you will be carried on a stretcher to your post-mission medical check-up.

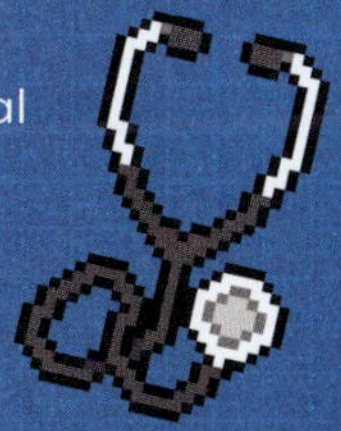

Emergency landing:
WHAT TO WEAR

On your return to Earth, you might have to put on a hydrosuit. The suit protects you if you have an emergency landing on water, such as in the sea, a swamp or even in heavy snow. The suit is designed to support you in very cold conditions outside the spacecraft for up to 12 hours. If you are in the landing spacecraft, it could support you for about 3 days, alongside the emergency survival kit.

1 Hood

The hood keeps your head warm and protected from the wet and cold.

2 Inflatable collar

The inflatable collar is similar to the life jacket on an aeroplane. It has a mouthpiece, so you can add more air to it if needed.

3 Zip

The large metal zip on the front of the suit runs from top to bottom, allowing you to get the suit on quickly in an emergency.

4 Rubber cuffs

Rubberised cuffs make sure the suit stays waterproof in all conditions. You also wear gloves to keep your hands dry.

5 Heavy material

The suit is made from heavy nylon material to keep you warm and dry.

6 Pockets

Velcro® pockets are useful for storing essential equipment.

7 Boots

The laced-up rubber-soled boots on the outside of the suit keep the suit waterproof and allow a good fit around your feet.

Forel hydrosuit >
a Russian-designed emergency suit for landing in water

EMERGENCY RESCUE

Mission Control monitors your return from space and makes sure everything is going to plan. However, your spacecraft might not land where expected. When this happens, you'll need to put your survival training into practice until you are rescued.

Astronaut rescue agreement

A treaty is a legal written agreement between different countries or organisations. To make sure that astronauts were kept safe and given help in the event of an unexpected landing in a different country, a treaty called the Rescue Agreement was created in 1967. This means that if you were to have an unexpected landing, the country you land in would be expected to help with rescue efforts and getting you back safely to your launching country.

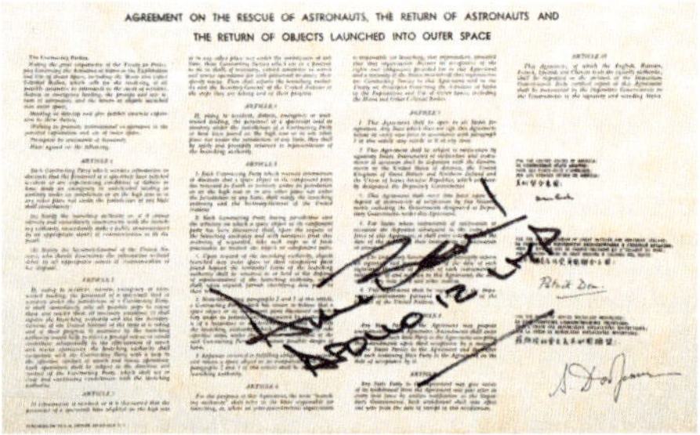
AGREEMENT ON THE RESCUE OF ASTRONAUTS, THE RETURN OF ASTRONAUTS AND THE RETURN OF OBJECTS LAUNCHED INTO OUTER SPACE

Priorities for an emergency landing

1 Safety and protection

Check yourself and your crew for injuries and provide first-aid if needed. Use the spacecraft and available materials to make a shelter.

2 Assess and signal

Check the spacecraft for damage, especially if it's an emergency splash landing. Is it sealed? Use beacons, flares and radios to communicate your location and help the search and rescue team find you.

3 Survival strategies

Use your emergency food and drink rations, and put your critical survival skills into action while waiting for rescue, such as making a fire to keep warm.

Case study > Soyuz 23 mission

In 1976, two cosmonauts, Vyacheslav Zudov and Valery Rozhdestvensky, made a dangerous emergency splashdown when their Soyuz 23 mission didn't go as expected. They launched and attempted to dock with a Soviet space station called Salyut 5. The system to guide their docking failed, and they had to make an early return to Earth. This unexpected return resulted in the spacecraft landing in Lake Tengiz, in Kazakhstan, in –20°C!

CASE STUDY

How the rescue unfolded

1 Stuck in the water

The parachute that slowed their return as they fell back to Earth submerged under the water and acted like an anchor, preventing them from moving.

2 Poor visibility

The rescue was particularly challenging because it was night-time and there were snowstorms.

3 Freezing conditions

The spacecraft had partly filled with water and it was losing heating power, so both cosmonauts were very cold.

4 Dangerous levels of CO_2

Carbon dioxide levels had also sharply increased in the closed spacecraft, causing the cosmonauts to feel drowsy and unable to concentrate. The crew spent around 10 hours in the capsule before being rescued.

Be prepared!

Several emergency rescues happened in the 1960s and 1970s, when spaceflight was relatively new. In more recent times, fewer rescues have been needed. However, as you've learned, space travel is full of hazards and it's always better to be prepared!

READJUSTING TO EARTH

You'll notice a few immediate differences as you begin to re-adjust to being back on Earth, such as different smells, changes in your vision, and how tricky it is to walk! You'll probably be carried out of your spacecraft after landing, because your body needs to get used to Earth's gravity again. You might make a quick call to a loved one, and smile for the rescue team and news crews who are there to celebrate your return.

It's good to be back!

You may notice how the air, soil, grass and even the ocean smell strong and wonderful! After being stuck on the ISS for months, where the environment smells like a combination of a hospital (antiseptic and clinical) and a railyard (hot and metallic), natural scents from Earth are a welcome change.

Getting used to gravity

You'll probably struggle to stand, walk and stabilise your vision as your body starts to respond to the Earth's strong gravitational pull again. However, the six-month 'stuffy cold' you couldn't seem to shake (due to fluids collecting in the upper body in microgravity) will finally disappear!

Funny feelings

Tim Peake shared that he could feel the weight of his lips and tongue when he landed back on Earth. He had to change how he was talking!

Quarantine

Apollo astronauts who travelled to the Moon spent three weeks in quarantine (kept away from others) when they returned. This was mainly to make sure that they hadn't brought back an extra-terrestrial illness that could spread to other people. Astronauts who are returning from the ISS don't have strict quarantine periods, but you'll be monitored closely for medical reasons after landing. You'll have a few immediate post-flight check-ups and then you'll be allowed to go home. You might have to limit contact with other people (beyond close family) for a few weeks, in order to protect your immune system as you recover from your mission.

Quarantine press conference > astronauts from Expedition 73 pose for photos while in quarantine

HOME SWEET HOME

After six long months on the ISS, you've no doubt missed your home comforts! Now that you've arrived back home, what are you looking forward to the most?

A reunion with friends and family

After half a year away, with video calls being your only form of communication, you'll be eager to rush home once you're checked over and considered medically fit.

Who would you look forward to seeing the most?

Fresh air and nature

The living and working areas of the ISS are larger than a six-bedroom house. That's big, but if you weren't able to leave that house for six months, you'd probably be eager to get some fresh air! On your return to Earth, you'll have a renewed appreciation for nature and spending time outdoors.

Your own bed

While sleeping in microgravity is comfortable for the body, it does lack a certain cosiness. You should enjoy sleeping horizontally on a mattress again and snuggling under some blankets.

Hot showers

Wet wipes, sponge baths and no-rinse shampoo have been as close to bathing as you've got during your stay on the ISS. Having a hot shower with running water is something returning astronauts very much look forward to.

'Real' food

With a menu of dried, rehydratable and canned foods making up most meals on the ISS, most astronauts miss having fresh fruit, vegetables and salads. Besides the healthy stuff, you may also look forward to chomping on fresh bread, pizza and foods that are crunchy and spicy!

What would your first meal back on Earth be?

RECOVERY AND REHABILITATION

When you return from the ISS, you'll undergo an official rehabilitation programme that lasts one to two months – but a full recovery can take many more! Rehabilitation includes checking for changes to your heart, muscles and bone density, and is necessary to help you get used to being in Earth's gravity again.

0-3 days

You'll focus on overcoming initial dizziness and balance issues, while your body gets used to Earth's gravity again.

2 weeks

Because the heart muscles weaken in space and blood pressure drops when you return to Earth, you might feel lightheaded, and it can take a couple of weeks to re-adjust.

1-3 months

Muscle mass and strength generally recover, helped by intense and supervised workouts over several months.

6 months and beyond

You may never fully recover from some health changes, like bone density loss. You'll continue with different types of therapy and specialised exercises to return to as close to full health as possible.

The recovery programme

Your recovery programme isn't just about physical improvement; it's designed to help you return to a normal life on Earth once again. You will receive a wide range of support.

1 Physical training

For about two hours every day, you'll focus on slowly building up your strength, endurance and heart health.

2 Restoring daily abilities

You'll do pool-based training and walking exercises to restore your standing and sitting posture, your gait (how you walk) and your agility (how quickly and easily you move).

3 Balance and coordination

You'll work through targeted exercises that re-train the inner ear system, to manage dizziness and improve your balance.

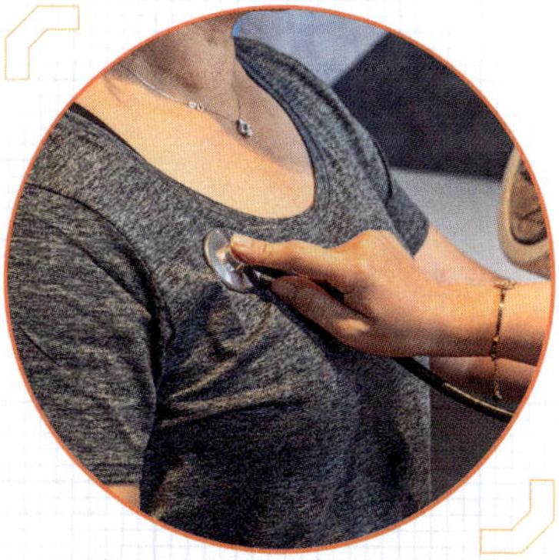

4 Targeted exercise

Over several months, you'll use special equipment to help rebuild your muscle mass and strengthen your bones.

5 Medical monitoring

You'll have regular checks for vision changes, heart health and nutrition levels to make sure your body recovers as well as possible.

6 Counselling

You'll be monitored for mental health and how you re-adapt to normal life.

LIFE AFTER SPACE

Your mission is drawing to a close. As you complete your recovery and rehabilitation, you'll spend some time de-briefing and providing feedback to the many teams on the ground who supported your mission. But what comes next?

CAPCOM in Mission Control

Do you work well under pressure? CAPCOM, the Capsule Communicator, is the only person in Mission Control who directly speaks to the astronauts in space. Their job is to pass on any instructions and information, and provide clear communication. Having trained and potentially been on a space mission themselves, they provide a trusted voice to represent the crew's needs to the Mission Control team.

Astronaut Trainer

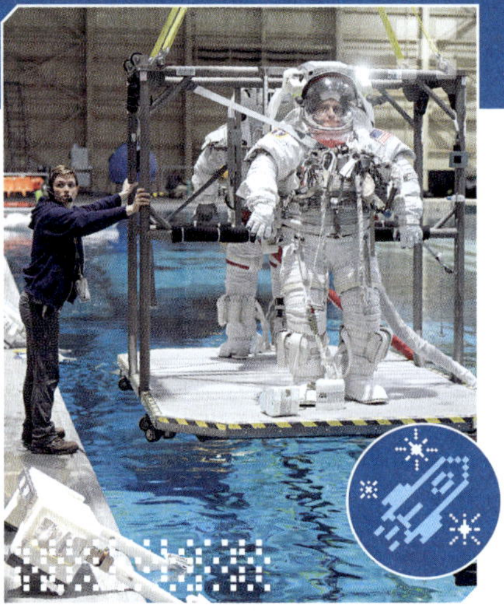

Do you enjoy teaching and helping others? As an experienced astronaut, you could help train future crews using simulators and underwater facilities that mimic microgravity. After returning from space, many astronauts use their skills and abilities to get the next generation of space travellers ready for the challenges of a mission.

Space Chef

Do you enjoy cooking? As a space chef, you would need to plan a space menu that meets the strict safety and hygiene standards required for space. You would also have to be imaginative with available ingredients to create nutritious and tasty meals for astronauts and space travellers.

Technical Expert

Are you creative and a good team player? In your training, during your launch and landing, and while on the ISS, you will have used many different technical and electrical systems. You could get involved in developing new spacecraft, systems or procedures that would make future spaceflights even better.

The Aerospace Industry

In addition to space agencies like NASA and ESA, there are many private and commercial space companies. You could work for one of them as a project manager, an engineer, a technician or even a safety inspector. It's even possible to work as an astronaut for a private company, like ex-NASA astronaut Peggy Whitson who joined Axiom Space as Director of Human Spaceflight.

DIY Space Experiment:

MAKE A PARACHUTE LANDER

Some spacecraft use parachutes to slow down on return to Earth. How do you think the size of the parachute might affect its return? Let's find out!

What you need:

- A plastic bag, e.g. a bin bag
- String
- 2 x yoghurt pots
- Sticky tape
- A weight, e.g. a small toy or a peg
- Scissors
- A ruler
- A pen
- A stopwatch

What to do:

1 Cut out your parachutes

Draw and then cut out two squares from the plastic bag – one should be 20 cm x 20 cm and the other should be 30 cm x 30 cm. These will be your parachutes.

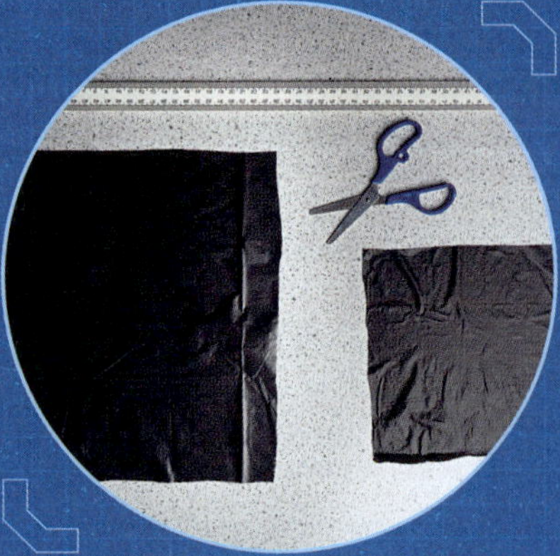

2 Attach the string

Cut eight pieces of string, each 25 cm long – four for each parachute. Use the sticky tape to attach the end of each piece of string to a corner of each parachute.

3 Attach the yoghurt pots

Attach the other end of each piece of string to one of the yoghurt pots, making sure these are evenly spaced. You should now have two parachute landers with different sized parachutes.

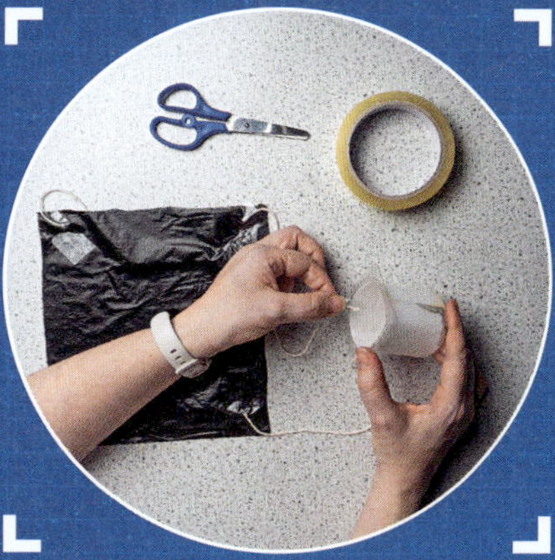

4 Add the weight

Put the weight (toy) inside the large parachute lander.

5 Find a drop zone

Now find a good spot to drop your landers from, a height of at least 3m would be best. Check with an adult before dropping them and have your stopwatch ready to time the landing.

6 Drop the large lander

Drop the large parachute lander. Make sure the parachute is fully open.

7 Repeat the drop

To get an average landing time, drop the lander three times, then add your times together and divide by three.

8 Drop the small lander

Now put the weight inside the small parachute lander and drop it three times to get an average landing time. Which parachute had the slowest landing?

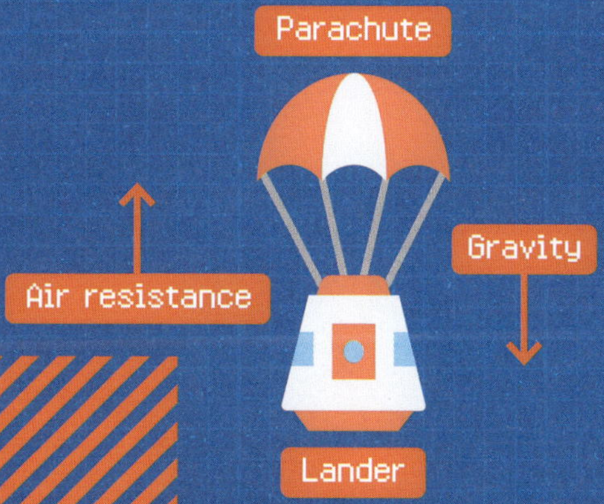

What's the science?

Just like rockets, gravity will pull a returning spacecraft back to Earth – but in this case, we need to slow it down, so it doesn't crash land. You should have found that the larger the surface area of the parachute, the slower the parachute lander fell. Parachutes use their large surface area to increase the air resistance or drag – this slows the lander down as it returns to the ground.

Mission Log:
[YOUR NEXT MISSION]

Now you're home and have re-adjusted to life on Earth, it's time to think about your next space adventure.

As you begin to explore options for your next mission, you might want to think about...

> Where you will go next
> Future space stations
> Space bases
> How to survive on the Moon
> How to survive on Mars
> Communicating in space
> Rockets of the future
> New spacesuit technology
> Making space sustainable
> Space jobs of the future

WHERE WILL YOU GO NEXT?

Whether you decide to stay on Earth or go on another space mission, it's useful to understand the distance between our planet and other places in space. How far away is the Moon, Mars and beyond?

Fact File: Moon

- Distance from Earth = 384,400 km
- Size = 3,476 km in diameter
- Type of object = moon
- Total number of visitors = 12 people landed, 16 people flew around
- Orbits the Earth

How far away is the Moon?

The Moon is the furthest place in space that astronauts have travelled to – so far! This natural satellite is a long way from Earth, about 384,400 kilometres. To reach the Moon isn't simple and takes around three days. It is a moving target for a rocket, because it is continually orbiting Earth, so you need to have a calculated curved path to get there. In the future, the Moon might be a stopping-off point on the journey to Mars or beyond.

Flight path to the Moon

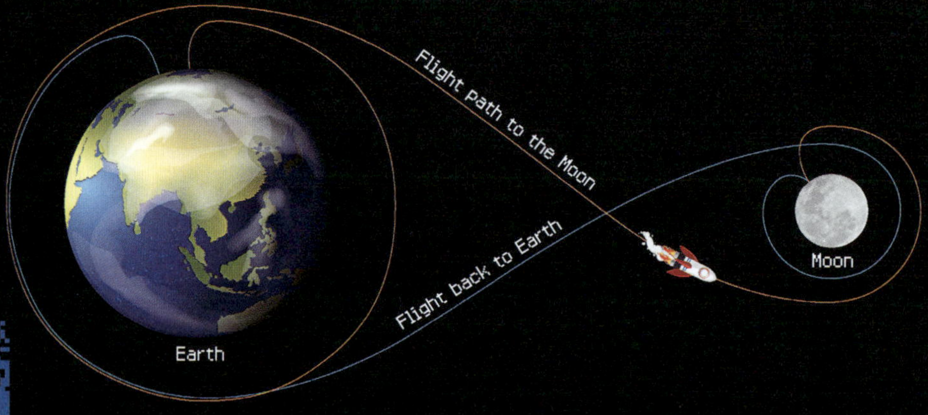

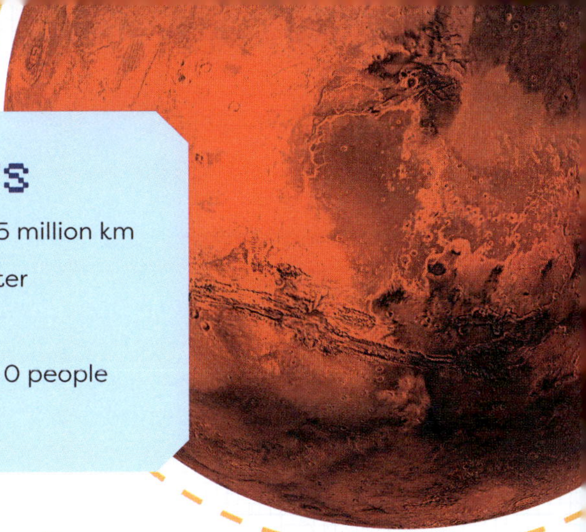

Fact File: Mars

- Distance from Earth = 225 million km
- Size = 6,779 km in diameter
- Type of object = planet
- Total number of visitors = 0 people
- Orbits the Sun

How far away is Mars?

Although Mars is on average 225 million kilometres away from Earth, there are times when the planets are closer and other times when they are further apart. Due to their oval-shaped orbits and because they are moving around the Sun at different speeds, their distance isn't fixed. Every 2–3 years the planets are at their closest distance, making it the best time to travel to Mars, but even then, the journey would still take 6–9 months!

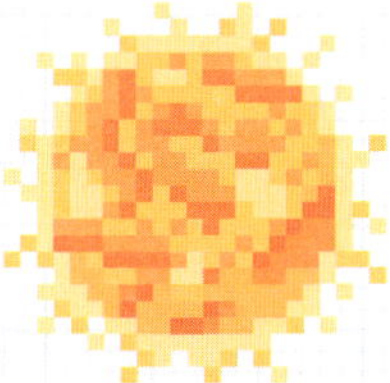

Are we there yet?

Astronomers and scientists use Astronomical Units (AU) to calculate distances in space, because they are dealing with such huge numbers. The distance between the Earth and the Sun is 1 AU, which is the same as 150 million kilometres! To travel this distance in a car at around 112 kilometres per hour would take nearly 150 years without stopping.

Beyond our Solar System

The spacecraft that has travelled furthest through space is Voyager 1. It's over 160 AU from Earth, moving at about 17 kilometres per second, or 3.5 AU per year. It launched in 1977, made its way past Jupiter and Saturn as it travelled towards the outer edges of the Solar System, and is now over 24 billion kilometres away from Earth! Currently we can only explore moons, planets and stars beyond our Solar System by using space telescopes. In the future, might we be able to travel the vast distances to these unexplored worlds?

FUTURE SPACE STATIONS

The ISS is beginning to age and needs a lot of maintenance and repairs, so it will be decommissioned (taken out of use) in 2030 and a spacecraft will be used to help de-orbit it in 2031. It will be directed to crash into a remote area of the South Pacific Ocean, likely burning up in Earth's atmosphere as it falls back towards our planet. What are the space stations of the future going to be like? If you decide to go on another space mission, which space station might you visit next?

Commercial space stations

There is likely to be a shift from government space stations, like the ISS and the Chinese Tiangong space station, to commercial space stations – ones developed and run by private companies.

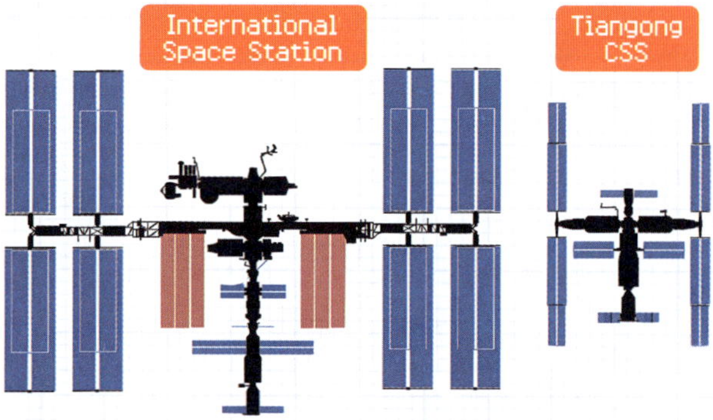

Axiom Station

Some future commercial space stations, like Axiom Station, are developing modules which will initially attach to the ISS before it is decommissioned. Once tested and checked, the modules will detach to become standalone structures.

Haven-1

Other space stations, like Haven-1 from a company called Vast, are getting ready to launch a single-module space station. At 10.1 metres long and 4.4 metres across, Haven-1 will be big enough for a few astronauts, but small enough to fit on a rocket for launch.

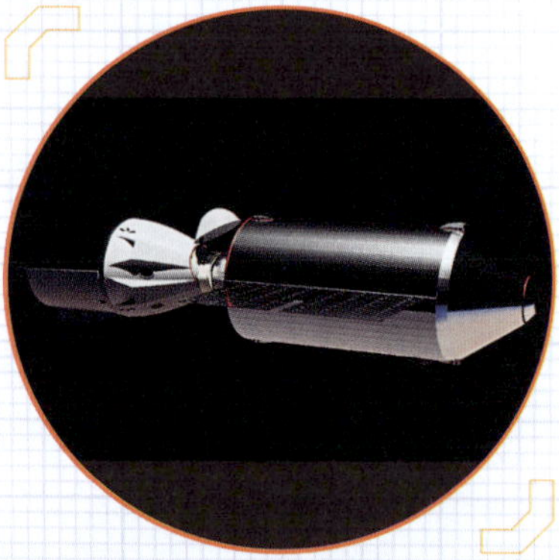

Research space stations

The main aim of current government space stations is scientific research and technology development. The ISS is involved in thousands of research experiments and investigations.

Tourist space stations

As commercial space stations begin to be built, another use will be for tourism. There have already been a few 'space tourists' on the ISS, but imagine something like a space hotel, with views out into the cosmos rather than of a beach! Not everyone wants to be an astronaut, but they might be willing to pay for a holiday in space, with some extra comforts that the ISS doesn't currently have.

Spaceport space stations

Some future space stations may act as a docking 'port' for spacecraft and landers, to make long-term exploration of the Moon and beyond easier. Just as people head to an airport to travel to different places, spaceport space stations will be a meeting point for incoming and outgoing missions.

SPACE BASES IN THE FUTURE

The future of space exploration looks exciting! You may be able to visit places far away, so you'll need to stay in a space station, Moon base or Martian habitat for long periods of time. If you decide to explore these worlds, you'll need life support systems, food and water. What will the space bases of the future be like?

The Moon

The Moon should be the perfect place for a space base – it is relatively close to Earth and could be a stopping-off point on the journey to Mars. There are some things to consider before this is possible:

Where to build

The lunar South Pole would make an ideal base on the Moon, because it has lots of sunlight and potential for good communication links to Earth.

Thin atmosphere

The Moon does not have breathable air, so a base would need to provide life support systems for astronauts. It also means the surface is hit by many meteoroids, which create the craters you can see across its surface – any habitats would need to be protected against possible impacts.

Water supplies

Shadowed craters in the lunar poles could potentially contain water ice that could be collected and used by astronauts.

Mars

Could we build a base on Mars? It's about half the size of Earth and has a similar surface and land features. Further away than the Moon, there are even more things to consider:

Lots to learn

First of all, we need to discover more about Mars before humans can build a base there! This will also help scientists understand the history of the Solar System, and even the origins of Earth.

Harsh environment

The potential for meteoroid impacts is high, there are extreme temperatures, as well as high levels of radiation that can be dangerous for humans.

Make it safe

Some scientists have suggested building cave-type hobbit holes as shelters for astronauts, to provide protection from the challenging conditions.

SURVIVING ON THE MOON

Your first taste of space travel has been a mission to the ISS, but this could be just the start! As you've been finding out, humans are planning to return to the Moon, and this time stay there for longer periods of time, not just a few days. It won't be possible to make frequent trips from Earth to bring new supplies – astronauts will need to be resourceful in order to live and work there.

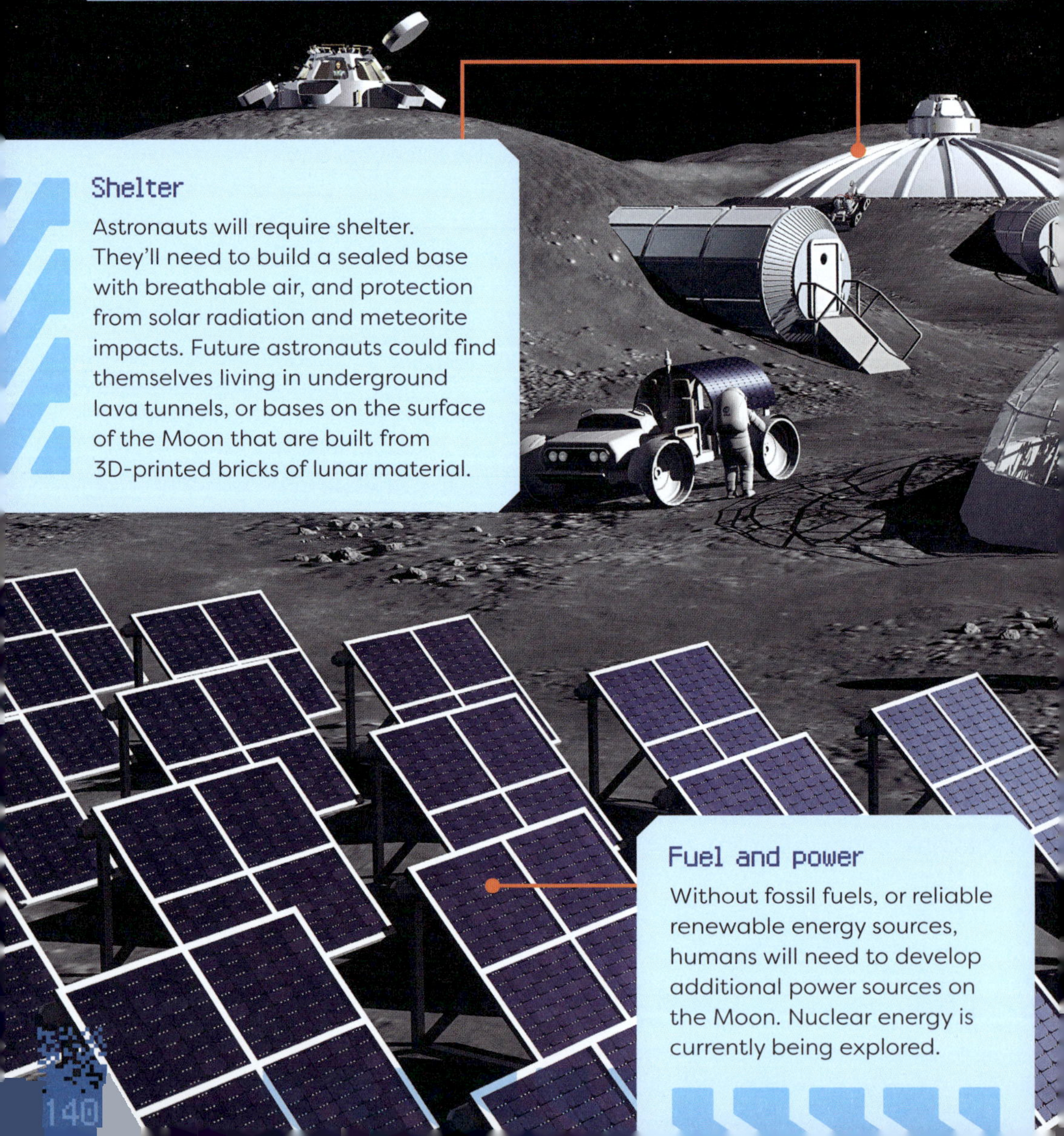

Shelter

Astronauts will require shelter. They'll need to build a sealed base with breathable air, and protection from solar radiation and meteorite impacts. Future astronauts could find themselves living in underground lava tunnels, or bases on the surface of the Moon that are built from 3D-printed bricks of lunar material.

Fuel and power

Without fossil fuels, or reliable renewable energy sources, humans will need to develop additional power sources on the Moon. Nuclear energy is currently being explored.

Water

The Moon doesn't have any liquid water on its surface, but spacecraft orbiting the Moon have calculated that there is enough water ice at the lunar poles to fill at least 240,000 Olympic-sized swimming pools! How will astronauts collect this frozen water to use for drinking and other requirements?

Food

The Moon doesn't have nutrient-rich soil to grow food. So astronauts will need to build on the knowledge gained from growing plants on the ISS to develop specially designed greenhouses, or enclosed habitats. These will hopefully provide the necessary conditions for crops and plants to grow.

SURVIVING ON MARS

There will be even more challenges to overcome if you travel to Mars. The journey will take six months or more. When you arrive, life there is likely to be difficult because of the thin atmosphere of mainly carbon dioxide and nitrogen, the cold temperatures and the desert-like environment, without any liquid water supplies. This all means that visitors to Mars will need help from technology.

High-tech spacesuits

Astronauts will need spacesuits that are comfortable, functional and able to keep them safe and protected from the harsh Mars environment.

Powerful rockets

Powerful propulsion systems for rockets and spacecraft will help get astronauts to Mars and back quicker!

Inflatable heat shields

Heat shields could fold up to take up less space in a rocket. Then, they'll unfold on Mars to protect the crew as they make their way to the planet's surface.

Inflatable heat shield >
being developed by scientists at NASA

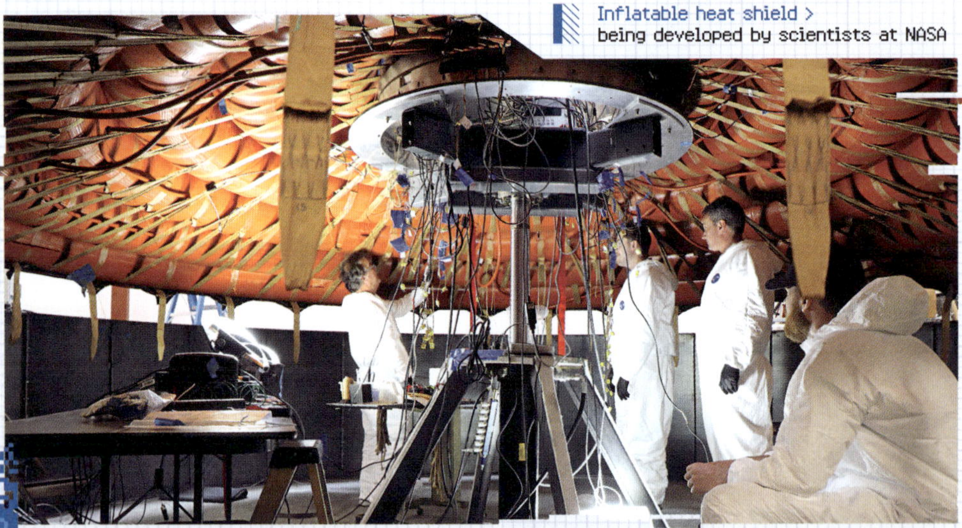

Mars motor home

The first missions will combine a base or Martian home with a roving vehicle to minimise the number of things that astronauts need to take to Mars. Like a motor home, the roving vehicle will have everything inside it to allow astronauts to live and work for weeks.

COMMUNICATING IN SPACE

If you are going to explore further out in space, you'll need to overcome communication issues. Spacecraft and astronauts have to be able to receive orders from Earth, send back information, and also get data from other satellites. Communicating across the large distances in space brings unique challenges!

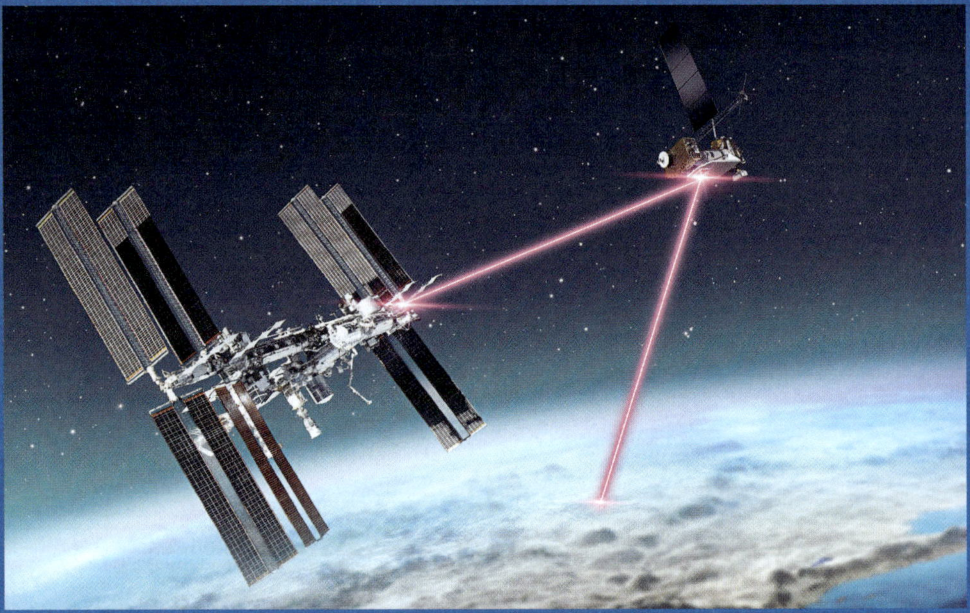

Long delays

Most communication uses a form of light, like invisible radio waves, to send a signal. Even though light travels at the fastest possible speed (about 300,000 kilometres per second!), it still takes a little time to get a message somewhere across space, because things are so far apart. For example, a signal to the Moon takes 1.25 seconds to get there from Earth. So if you're waiting for a reply, that's a 2.5-second delay. Depending on where Mars is in its orbit, the delay can be anywhere from 4 to 24 minutes – and twice that long if you're waiting for a response!

Staying connected

You'll need to accept that real-time communication, like instant phone calls, won't be possible for deep space missions. Instead, you'll have to rely on emails and file transfers that have a delay in response. Other forms of communication are being developed for communicating in space – laser communication, relay satellites and the interplanetary internet.

Laser communication

Radio wave signals like those used in mobile phones can work in all weather conditions. Laser communication is better for communicating large amounts of information, though it can be affected by clouds. So it's likely that future space communication technology will need to make use of both of these.

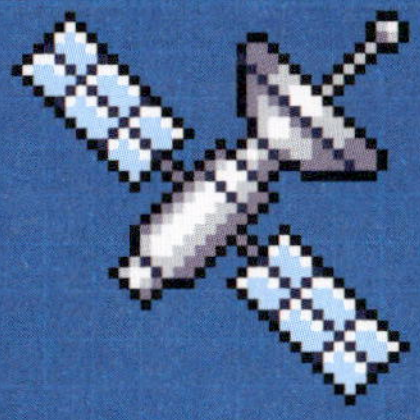

Relay satellites

A person running around an athletic track may tire towards the end of a race. In the same way, a signal travelling long distances in space will weaken. But in a relay race, each runner only travels a part of the total distance and can maintain their strength. Similarly, a series of relay satellites can work together to help improve communication.

The interplanetary internet

Because things in space are always moving, communication links aren't always in the right place to pass on a message. The interplanetary internet works by packing up information (like a parcel). Each spacecraft or satellite saves the data until they can pass it on. Messages 'hop' from one place to the next, and if one link is down, the message is re-sent later – similar to a driver attempting to re-deliver your parcel if you aren't at home! Even though the communication isn't instant, it is reliable.

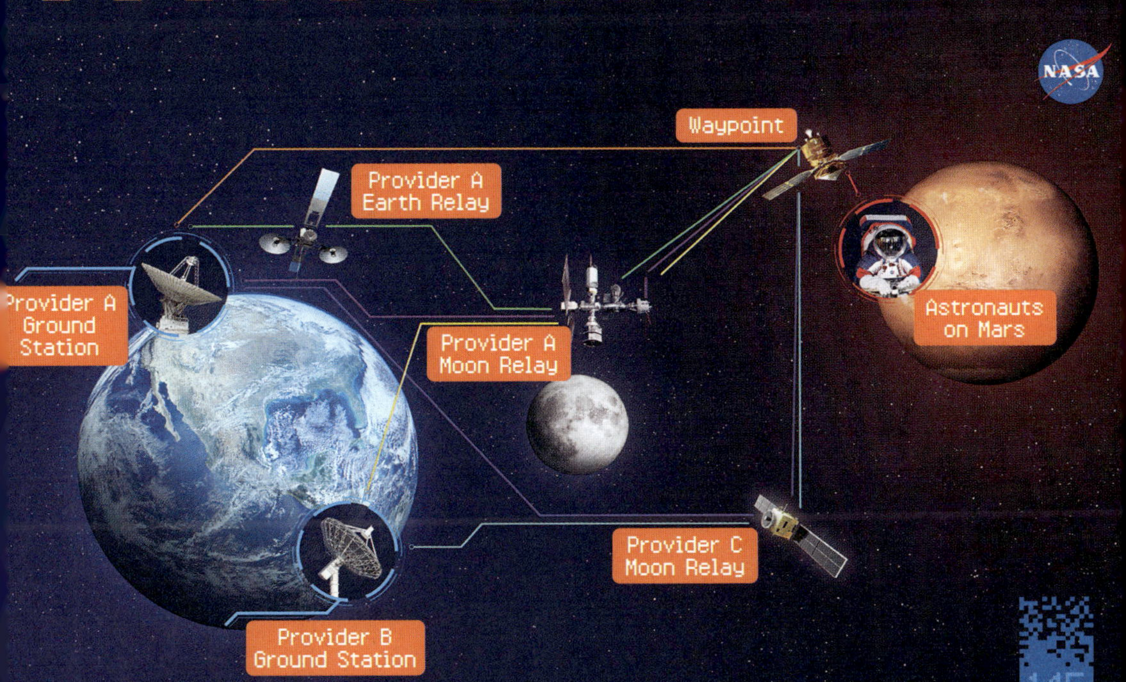

FUTURE ROCKETS

If you decide to go on another space adventure, the rocket you travel in is likely to be different from what you're used to. Future rockets will have to travel vast distances – this means that they will need more space for a larger crew, and for the supplies and equipment needed for the journey. So how are future rockets being designed?

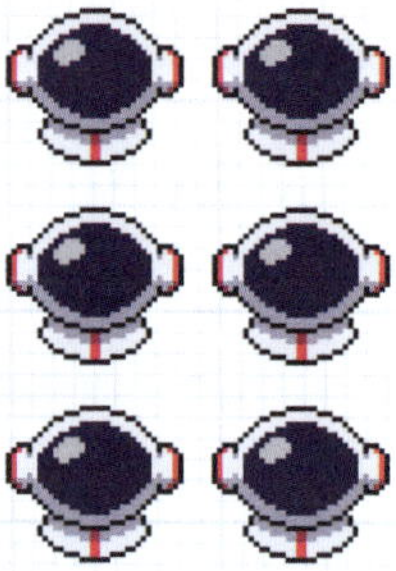

Larger crews

Longer journeys into space will require a larger crew, to help with things like medical issues, repairs and communication. Exploring new areas will also mean that more specialist astronauts are needed on missions. Current missions to the ISS take three or four astronauts, but it is likely that missions to Mars will require crews of six or more, and rockets will need to be designed accordingly.

Longer trips

Spacecraft will need to be comfortable for astronauts to travel on long journeys. More room will be needed for food and water, as well as for equipment for things like recycling waste. Long flights will result in astronauts losing bone density and muscle unless they exercise, but the large exercise equipment used on the ISS won't fit on current rockets. More compact and efficient exercise equipment will need to be designed for long journeys. This may include compression suits to support heart health and blood flow, and equipment that can be used in a seated position.

Fuel

Future space rockets will also need more fuel for longer trips. Most of the fuel used in space travel is needed for launch, to overcome gravity and reach launch speed. However, even small manoeuvres in space require some fuel, and rockets will need more space for it.

3D-printable parts

It is already possible to 3D print metal parts of a rocket, such as the thrusters, and in some cases, this is cheaper than more traditional methods. In the future, it should be possible to 3D print any parts needed for the rocket, to make repairs simpler and easier to complete.

Roomy rockets!

In the past, it has been important to have large rockets, such as the Space Shuttle, to launch modules of the ISS to space. In the future, it will also be important for rockets to be able to transport large equipment. They may not have to carry fully built parts of a habitat, but they will need to supply the building materials for 3D printing, as well as equipment to design and print parts. Rockets will also need to take supplies, such as food, water and recycling systems, to habitats of the future on the Moon or Mars, on separate missions. This will be a bit like a space delivery service!

What do you think a future rocket to Mars should look like?

SPACESUITS OF THE FUTURE

Spacesuits of the future will need to have the same life support systems, temperature controls, cameras, visors and equipment as the EVA suits that astronauts wear now. However, they'll also need to withstand harsher environments and last for longer than the suits used on the ISS. So how will they be different?

Radiation protection

The Moon and Mars have thin atmospheres – the high radiation levels can damage clothing and harm your body. The outer material of your spacesuit must be able to protect you from this harsh environment. In 2020, the Perseverance rover took a special instrument to Mars known as SHERLOC, which included five different materials to be tested in the harsh environment. The outcome of this experiment will help decide which are the best spacesuit materials to use for future missions.

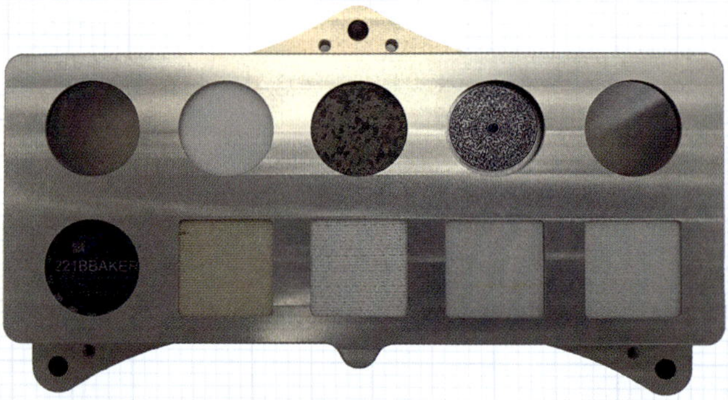

SHERLOC >
Perseverance instrument

Tough stuff

The surfaces of the Moon and Mars are covered in a dusty, rocky layer called regolith, which can wear down materials. On Mars, the dust is sometimes whipped up by winds on the surface, damaging equipment, habitats and spacesuits. So any future spacesuits will need to be made of tough stuff!

Good mobility

On the ISS, you are mostly floating, so you need good movement in your hands and arms. But on the Moon and Mars, it will be important that your whole body, including your legs and torso, has good mobility. This means that the suit will need to be designed to have more bend and flex. The Axiom Extravehicular Mobility Unit, or AxEMU, is currently being developed. This spacesuit has been designed to withstand the harsh conditions of the Moon and Mars. It has flexibility around the knees to help astronauts complete their work.

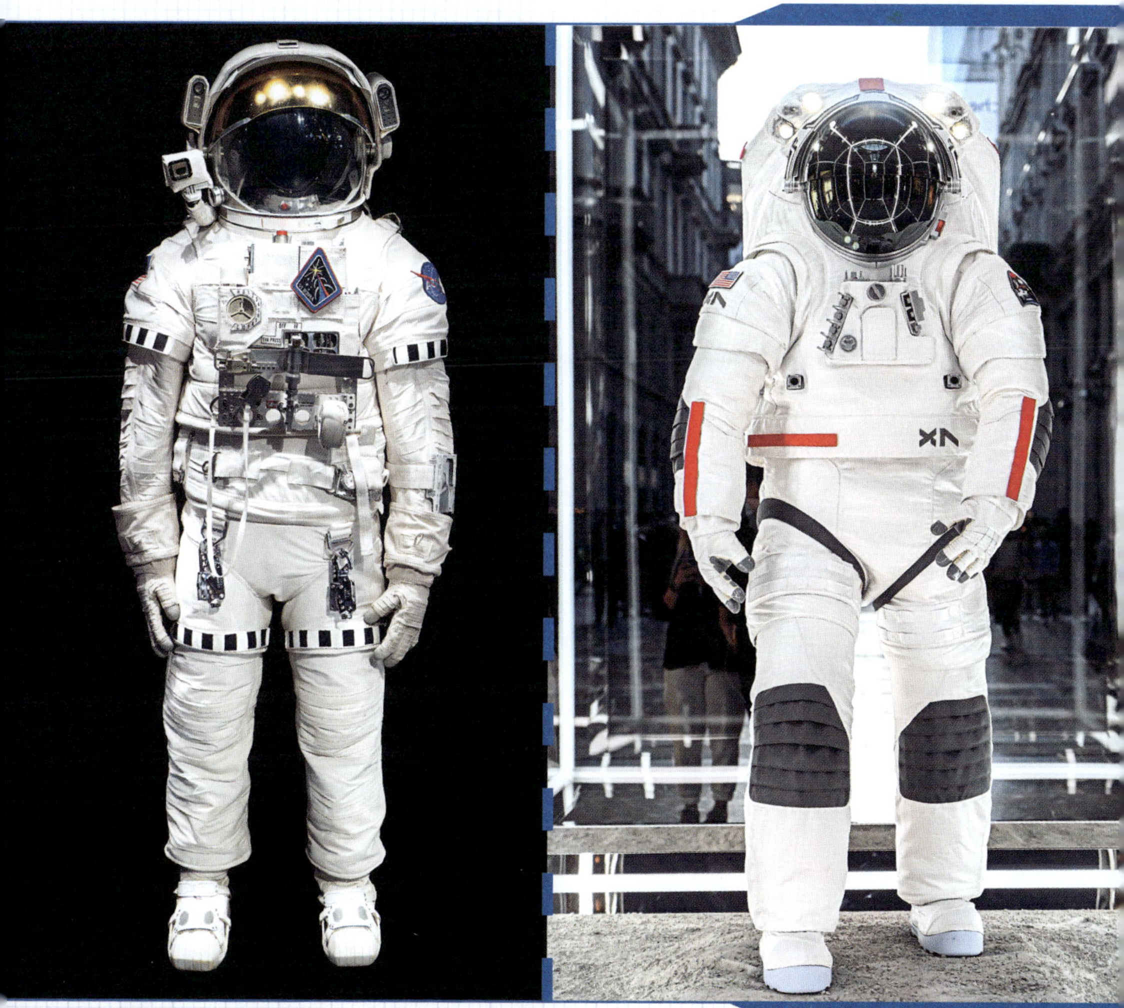

Left > EVA spacesuit from The Martian film
Right > AxEMU (Axiom Extravehicular Mobility Unit)

Tool belt

This is the spacesuit worn in the film The Martian. It has a tool belt which holds equipment you might need to use when working on Mars. What tools might you need on Mars?

Footwear

Footwear will need to be strong to withstand the harsh, rocky surfaces of the Moon and Mars. Both places are mainly dry, but the rocks and debris will make walking a challenge.

MAKING SPACE SUSTAINABLE

Travelling and living vast distances from Earth will be expensive and use lots of resources. So scientists need to look at sustainable options to reduce costs and the amount of things that need to be transported. This is being done in a variety of ways.

Fuel

Scientists are already looking at more sustainable fuel options for the future. By using renewable energy supplies from waste materials from plants, animal feed and vegetables, sustainable fuels can be used in rockets instead of fossil fuels. Some scientists believe that using resources found on other planets and the Moon, such as Helium-3, could be another way of fuelling spacecraft of the future. However, more research is needed to see how this can be done.

Recycling

As you've seen, the ISS already recycles water, air and packaging. It will be even more important to recycle these things on the Moon and Mars. While astronauts are waiting for supplies from Earth, they will need to be self-sufficient. Some scientists have suggested using human poo as a fertiliser for plants in space!

Debris

Increasing the number of launches to space is likely to increase the amount of space debris left behind; it might make some areas in Earth's orbit completely unusable. To make space more sustainable, scientists need to find ways to reduce or collect this debris. Space agencies such as ESA and NASA are working towards a 'Zero Debris Approach' – this means that future missions will not create any debris. There are also stricter rules for new launches, such as returning satellites to Earth within five years of the end of their life. This avoids collisions and prevents the release of small particles into the atmosphere.

3D printing

3D printing processes are being tested to see if they can be used for things like tools, equipment and small fixings. Being able to 3D print these kinds of items will save space, weight and costs for launch, because you'll only print the equipment you require as you need it. Here is NASA astronaut, Jeanette Epps, using a 3D printer to produce experimental samples from stainless steel.

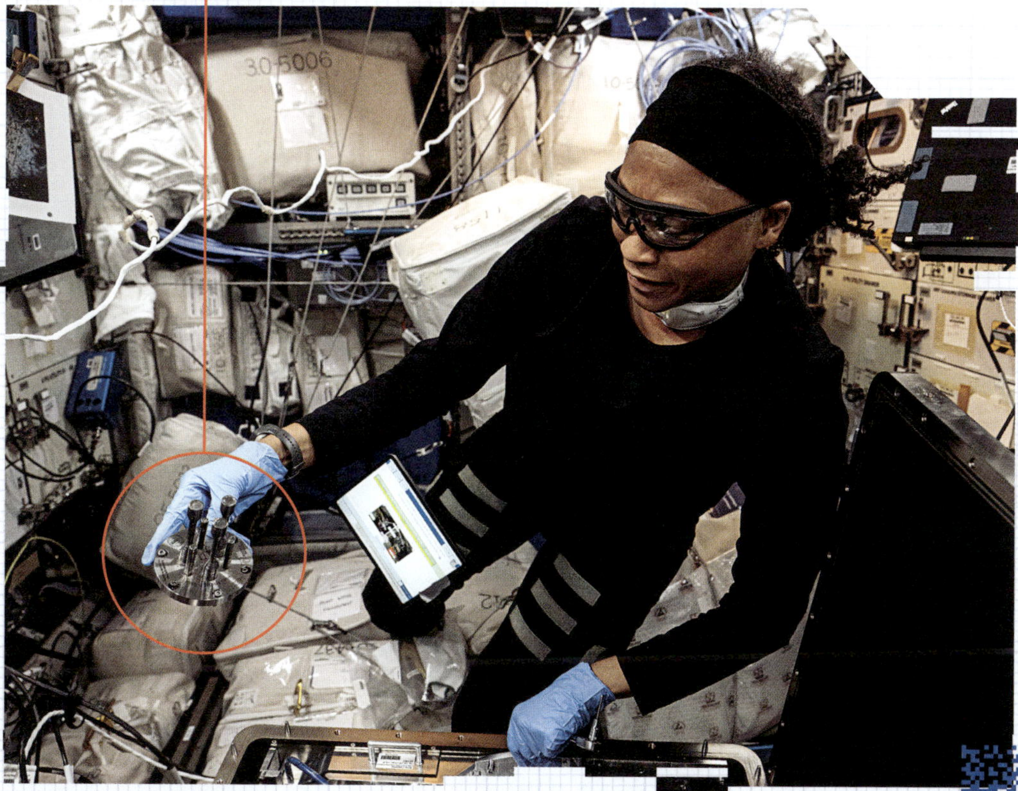

SPACE JOBS OF THE FUTURE

With space exploration developing at a fast rate, a range of new careers are likely to become essential in the future. Could you see yourself taking on any of these roles?

Space Doctor/ Astro-pharmacist

As part of your astronaut training programme, you did basic medical training, and there is some medical equipment on the ISS to help if a crew member becomes ill. In an emergency, you can return to Earth in a few hours. However, for managing health on long flights to the Moon and Mars, space doctors and astro-pharmacists will need to join crews on their space missions.

Space Traffic Controller

Space is becoming more crowded – there are an increasing number of satellites and missions launching, and also a growing amount of space debris. To help prevent collisions and manage the 'space superhighway', space traffic controllers will be needed, a bit like air traffic controllers who manage incoming and outgoing flights at airports.

Space Tourism Operator

As space stations begin to cater to holidaying space travellers, space tourism operators will need to manage different aspects of a visitor's stay in space. On Earth, operators are required to manage bookings, and tell customers about activities and places to eat. What kinds of things might space tourism operators need to organise?

Space Architect

On long-term space missions to the Moon and Mars, astronauts will need somewhere to stay – you could help design their temporary homes! A space architect will need to think about the challenges of the environment, what materials are available to use and the practical requirements of an astronaut's home.

Space Politician

Space exploration is growing and changing very quickly. So it's important that we have rules and regulations in place to make sure space remains sustainable and safe for everyone to explore. If you are responsible, resilient and organised, you may enjoy working in government and helping to develop space laws that don't yet exist!

DIY Space Experiment:

DESIGN A SPACE STATION

Have a go at creating your own space station of the future! What will it look like, how will it be used and what will you take with you on your next mission?

What you need:

- Cardboard tubes, like kitchen roll
- Paper
- Scissors
- Glue/tape
- Colouring pens or pencils
- Paper straws

What to do:

1 Pick your space station

Decide what type of space station you want to make – for example, a research station, a spaceport or a space tourism hub.

2 Pick your modules

Decide how many modules you want your space station to have. You'll need one cardboard tube for each module, and you can create as many as you like. Make sure your space station has all the modules it needs. For example, will you have modules for living and working in, for storage, docking, research, or even a viewing area?

3 Get creative

Decorate the tubes to look like the outside of a space station. You could draw windows, airlocks, astronauts, cables, pipes, etc.

4 Attach the solar panels

Make two holes in the middle of each tube with a pencil and push through a paper straw. For each module, cut out two paper rectangle shapes. Use the tape to stick one rectangle on each end of the straw – these are your solar panels.

5 Add a link module

Crumple a piece of paper to make a paper ball. At the end of one of the tubes, attach the paper ball with either glue or tape. This ball represents a link module, that connects separate modules together – just like a door between rooms on Earth.

6 Keep on building

Now, attach two more modules to the link module, one in each direction. This makes three modules in total. You'll need to attach another paper ball (link module) to one of the tubes if you've designed a station with more than three modules. Keep going until you've completed your space station!

What's next?

Once you've finished making your space station, think about what you'll need to take with you on your next mission. Which crew members will need to go with you? What equipment will be essential? And what personal belongings will you take along? Write a list or draw the things and stick them on!

Mission Log:
[FINAL ENTRY]

Congratulations, astronaut! You have successfully completed your first mission and are now set for your next adventure.

But don't forget, an astronaut's training is never complete - there is always more to learn about our amazing Universe. So be sure to take this handbook with you on your next journey into the stars.

Safe travels!

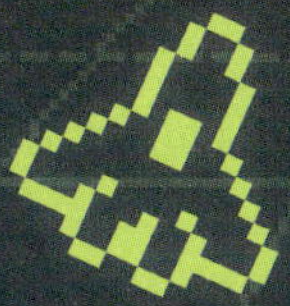

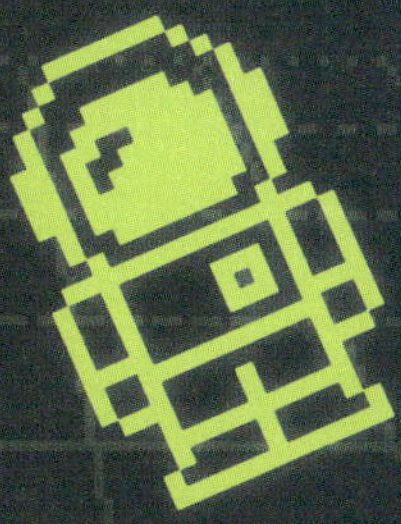

PHOTO CREDITS

Whilst every effort has been made to trace the copyright owners of the images used in this book, in cases where this has been unsuccessful, or if any have inadvertently been overlooked, the publishers would gladly receive any information enabling them to rectify any error or omission at the first opportunity.

p4 + back cover Meganne Christian portrait > © ESA - A. Conigli
p4 Antarctica > © Meganne Christian
p4 diving > © ESA - H. Stevenin
p5 floating > © ESA/Novespace-L.Theillet
p10 Eileen Collins > © NASA
p10 Jessica Watkins > © NASA/Bill Ingalls
p11 Charles Walker > © NASA
p11 Barbara Morgan > © NASA/Robert Markowitz
p11 Cai Xuzhe & Song Lingdong > © Xinhua/Alamy Stock Photo
p14 Principia patch > © Wilf Doyle/Alamy Stock Photo
p15 Tim Peake training suit > © Andrew Lloyd/Alamy Stock Photo
p16 air bladder > © Dmitry Zimin/Alamy Stock Photo
p17 high-altitude flight training suit > © National Space Centre
p18 spacecraft touch screen > © NASA
p19 astronauts with flags > © NASA/Jack Fischer
p20 underwater training > © NASA
p20 centrifuge > © NASA
p21 Vomit Comet > © NASA
p21 oxygen test > © ESA/DLR
p22 inside the Soyuz spacecraft > © NASA/Bill Ingalls
p23 John McFall (left) > © Andrew Wong/Stringer via Getty Images
p23 John McFall (right) > © ESA - A. Conigli
pp24-25 Mission Control > © NASA
p27 Christmas on the ISS > © NASA
p27 Chris Hadfield playing guitar > © EMU history/Alamy Stock Photo
p27 slime in space > © NASA
p28 sea survival > © ESA
p29 survival kit > © National Space Centre
p30 dexterity test > © National Space Centre
p33 reaction time test > © National Space Centre
p34 Artemis II SLS Rocket > © NASA/Brandon Hancock
p37 Saturn V rocket > © NASA
p37 Ariane 1 rocket > © ESA/CNES/ARIANESPACE - D. Ducros
p39 Ariane 5 rocket > © ESA/CNES/Arianespace
p41 SRBs > © NASA/Frank Michaux
p44 Soyuz TMA-9 spacecraft > © NASA/Bill Ingalls
p44 Soyuz 7K-OK spacecraft > © National Space Centre
p45 Space Shuttle Discovery > © NASA/KSC
p46 SpaceX Falcon 9 > © NASA/Joel Kowsky
p46 landing platform > © NASA/Bill Ingalls
p47 SpaceX Starship > © UPI/Alamy Stock Photo

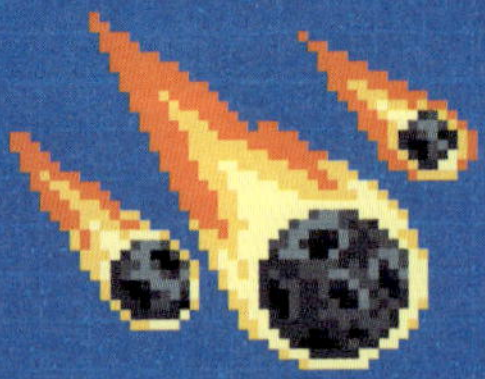

p47 New Glenn > © Sipa US/Alamy Stock Photo
pp48-49 activity photos > © National Space Centre
p53 quarantine > © NASA/Aubrey Gemignani
p53 health checks > © NASA/GCTC/Andrey Shelepin
p53 travel to launch pad > © NASA/Kim Shiflett
p55 Sokol KV-2 Rescue Spacesuit > © National Space Centre
p56 Possum's Fargo > © NASA/Jerry Ross
p57 Apollo 11 lunar module > © NASA
pp58-59 launch pad > © NASA/Jason Parrish
p60 astronauts getting into spacecraft > © NASA
p60 zero-G indicator > © NASA
p61 astronaut in spacecraft > © NASA/SpaceX
pp66-67 activity photos > © National Space Centre
p72 floating astronaut > © NASA
p72 ISS > © NASA
p73 treadmill > © NASA
p73 Earth from the ISS > © NASA/Takuya Onishi
p76 Advanced Resistive Exercise Device (ARED) > © NASA
p76 T2 COLBERT Treadmill > © NASA/Roman Romanenko
p77 Stationary Bike (CeVis) > © ESA/NASA
p77 Sunita Williams space triathlon > © NASA
p79 ISS toilet > © James Blair - NASA - JSC
p80 astronaut floating > © NASA
p80 haircut > © NASA
p81 shampoo > © NASA
p81 vacuuming > © NASA
p82 photography from the Cupola > © NASA
p82 personal space > © NASA/Koichi Wakata
p83 Christmas Eve on the ISS > © NASA
p83 gorilla suit > © Associated Press/Alamy Stock Photo
p83 football > © NASA
p84 sleeping area > © NASA
p85 astronauts sleeping > © NASA
p86 astronaut with water pouch > © ESA/NASA
p86 circular water > © NASA
p87 Refabricator > © NASA/MSFC/Emmett Given
p87 rubbish bags > © NASA
p88 circular water > © NASA
p89 drinking in microgravity > © NASA
p90 floating fruit > © ESA/NASA
p91 Great British Space Dinner > © National Space Centre
p91 food from around the world > © NASA
p92 astronaut eating > © NASA
pp92-93 activity photos > © National Space Centre
p94 astronaut on a spacewalk > © NASA
p96 cooling/ventilation layer > © NASA/Tom Trower
p97 Extravehicular Mobility Unit > © NASA/Robert Markowitz
p97 Snoopy cap > © James Blair - NASA - JSC
p98 astronaut performing repairs > © NASA
p99 astronaut tethering > © NASA
p100 bobtail squid > © NASA/Jamie S. Foster
p102 candles > © NASA
p103 growing specialised cells > © NASA/Shane Kimbrough

p103 space garden > © NASA/Cory Huston
p104 space debris around Earth > © NASA
p105 docked spacecraft > © NASA
p105 Kessler Syndrome > © ESA
p105 debris removal > © ESA-David Ducros, 2016
p106 astronaut using a biological printer > © NASA
p106 astronaut conducting an eye exam > © NASA/Karen Nyberg
p107 Mark and Scott Kelly > © Robert Markowitz - NASA - Johnson
p108 growing chilli peppers in space > © NASA/Kayla Barron
pp108-109 activity photos > © National Space Centre
p112 astronaut in hatch > © NASA/Bill Ingalls
p113 astronauts posing for a photo > © NASA
p114 spacecraft > © ESA/NASA
p115 heat shields > © ESA-M. Pedoussaut
p116 parachute > © ESA-Stephane Corvaja, 2015
p117 spacecraft recovery > © NASA/Bill Ingalls
p119 Forel hydrosuit > © National Space Centre
p120 Rescue Agreement > © National Space Centre
p120 emergency landing > © NASA/Bill Ingalls
p122 astronaut recovering > © NASA/Bill Ingalls
p122 astronaut waving > © ESA-Stephane Corvaja, 2016
p123 press conference in quarantine > © NASA/Joel Kowsky
p124 reunion with friends and family > © ESA-Philippe Sebirot, 2016
p126 thumbs up > © NASA/Keegan Barber
p128 CAPCOM > © NASA/Bill Stafford
p128 Astronaut Trainer > © NASA/James Blair
p129 Space Chef > © Richard Splash/Alamy Stock Photo
p129 Technical Expert > © NASA, David Bowman
p129 Aerospace Industry > © NASA/Joel Kowsky
p130 parachute lander > © NASA/Christopher LC Clark
pp130-131 activity photos > © National Space Centre
p135 Voyager 1 > © NASA/JPL-Caltech
p136 International Space Station/Tiangong CSS > © Thomas Shafee/CC-BY-4.0
p136 Axiom Station > © Axiom Space, Inc./CC-BY-SA-4.0
p136 Haven-1 > © Edits4019/CC-BY-4.0
p137 astronauts conducting research > © NASA
p137 spaceport space station > © NASA/Alberto Bertolin, Bradley Reynolds
p138 astronauts on the Moon > © NASA
pp140-141 Moon base > © ESA-P. Carril
p142 high-tech spacesuit > © NASA/Bill Stafford
p142 heat shield > © NASA/Langley Research Center
p143 Mars motor home > © NASA/BILL STAFFORD NASA-JSC HOUSTON T
p144 satellite laser links > © NASA
p145 interplanetary internet > © NASA
p146 spacecraft > © NASA/Terry White/SLS
p148 SHERLOC > © NASA/JPL-Caltech
p149 EVA spacesuit from The Martian > © National Space Centre
p151 3D printing (close-up) > © NASA/ESA/Airbus
p151 3D printing > © NASA
p153 Space Politician > © NASA/Bill Ingalls
pp154-155 activity photos > © National Space Centre
All other photos and illustrations > © Shutterstock